Hamlyn all-colour paperbacks

Peter Hinks

Jewellery

illustrated by Martin Battersby

Hamlyn · London
Sun Books · Melbourne

FOREWORD

The study of jewellery is an immense and complex one, and, in such a small space as this, one can only hope to sketch in the outlines, emphasising only those parts likely to be of interest to the average collector. Most of the collector's jewellery on the market is of the nineteenth century, but so much of this is derivative in design that some knowledge of earlier styles is essential to its proper understanding.

The goldsmith's techniques have changed only in detail since the time of the early Greeks. For this reason, it was felt that the section dealing with the working of precious metals would not be out of place near the beginning of the book, where it would explain many of the more obscure technical terms and processes referred to in the ensuing text. Many precious stones are of quite recent discovery, however, and consequently this section has been placed at the end of the book. As engraved gems are relevant to both the Classical period and to the Middle Ages, the pages on this subject have been placed between these two epochs. With these exceptions, the book follows a roughly chronological sequence.

I would like to express my thanks for the generous help given by Mr H. J. Ricketts, Mr G. D. Llewellyn and Miss Felicity Nicholson.

Peter Hinks

Published by The Hamlyn Publishing Group Limited
London · New York · Sydney · Toronto
Hamlyn House, Feltham, Middlesex, England
In association with Sun Books Pty Ltd Melbourne

Reprinted 1973

ISBN 0 600 00135 0

Phototypeset by Oliver Burridge Filmsetting Limited, Crawley, Sussex
Colour separations by Schwitter Limited, Zurich
Printed in England by Sir Joseph Causton & Sons Limited

CONTENTS

PRIMITIVE JEWELS

Primitive man decorated his body in many ways, all of them in use today. Dark-skinned people scored their bodies and rubbed in dung or caustic vegetable juices to produce a conspicuous pattern of scars. Other races introduced pigment through perforations in the skin: tattooing. Smearing with paint was neither so permanent nor so painful. Clothing is primarily functional, designed to protect the body from extremes of climate or to excite desire. The sexual element is also present in most forms of physical decoration and the distinction between jewellery and clothing is often blurred. Where do we place the superb collars and coronals of birds' plumage worn by Hawaiian chiefs or the plugs of rag in the ear-lobes of the Japanese Ainu? It is not enough to say that clothing is of soft, perishable materials and jewellery of hard, durable ones.

Seeds, nuts, seashells and small bones need only be drilled to make them into beads. Beads made of trout vertebrae have been found in European middens. Iridescent beetles are strung into beads in equatorial America, and pine nuts by the woodland Indians of the United States. In the beginning men made jewels from the objects nearest to hand but as trade developed materials became more dispersed.

White and purple shell beads, *wampum*, were used not only on the coast but by the Indians of the interior as well. Strung into necklaces and belts, they were used in tribal diplomacy as peace tokens, kept as historical records, or passed on as currency.

Beads in the form of a thin disc were made from suitable materials: shell in the South Seas, ostrich eggs in Africa. The material was first broken with a stone and fragments pierced and threaded on a stick. The whole thing was then ground to a smooth cylinder on a stone. This primitive mass-production method made beads of great regularity.

First and foremost jewellery has to be beautiful. Also, because it is a peculiarly intimate object, it should be precious. Trees are almost non-existent on barren Easter Island and wood was prized

Easter Island wood pendant

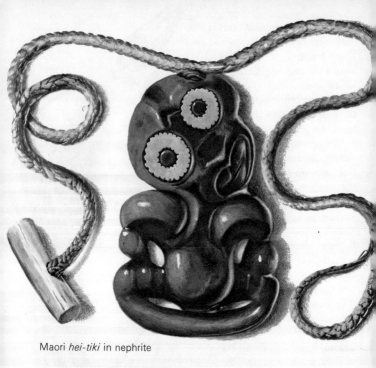

Maori *hei-tiki* in nephrite

so highly that the islanders used to make their jewellery from it. In order to waste as little material as possible, the design was adapted to the shape of the fragment and these curious figures of emaciated patriarchs, birds and lizards often take grotesque attitudes.

We must admire this primitive work for its beauty. Its technical excellence would be admirable even if made with steel tools, but when one considers that primitive man's implements were just shells, flakes of stone, rat's teeth, vegetable fibres and the like, his skill and patience must have been almost miraculous.

Holes were bored with the bow drill, an implement long in use for making fire, its shaft tipped with stone, or for harder materials with a paste of sand and water. Sawing was also accomplished with the bow by converting its fibre, or sinew, string to a cutting edge by coating it with abrasive.

The New Zealand Maori made their *hei-tiki* by string sawing. These curious foetus-like pendants, with their staring eyes of inlaid mother-of-pearl, made from flat pieces of the nephrite known as New Zealand jade, were handed down in the families of chiefs. Frequently they were worn only by alternate generations, being buried with their owner and then dug up by a grandchild. Another curious custom was for the wife of a captured chief to send her *hei-tiki* to the wife of his captor. *Hei-tikis* then were not only precious and beautiful ornaments but also badges of rank.

Another striking example was the hook-like pendant of whale ivory worn by a Hawaiian chief. This robustly graceful ornament was suspended by a hank of thin cords tightly braided from human hair. *Kap-kaps* are another Oceanic jewel of similar significance. These were made from a large disc of seashell decorated with tortoiseshell. In the Marquesas Islands, the decoration took a delicate curvilinear form; in the Solomon Islands, a spiky, angular design was followed.

Oceanic *kap-kaps* of shell with tortoiseshell decoration

Jewels also demonstrated the wearer's prowess as a hunter or fisherman. Necklaces could be made of jaguar's claws or of shark's teeth, and in New Guinea a woman would wear the claws of cassowaries killed by her husband during a hunting expedition.

Wealth, as well as courage, was shown off in the same way, and the shell currency of New Britain was sewn into huge collars and worn by men of substance. Obviously, wealth is not only displayed but stored in this way. Seeing an Indian peasant woman at a festival loaded with ornaments one might think she was a relatively wealthy person, whereas in all probability she would be wearing the entire family fortune.

Some primitive jewellery is so disfiguring that its object seems to have been to make the wearer ugly. In the case of the warrior this was probably so. Labrets, or lip-plugs, were often so heavy as to drag the lower lip down and expose the teeth when these were present. The Haida Indians of Queen Charlotte Island wore oblong labrets of wood finely inlaid with abalone shell. In Africa enormous labrets were worn in both lips, giving the owner the appearance of a duck and making eating and speaking a problem. Ear-plugs of similar proportions are also known and the giraffe-like collars worn by some African women are too well known to elaborate upon. It has been suggested that these grotesque ornaments were designed by men to make their women hideous and undesirable to marauders.

Jewellery was worn for advantage in combat. Warriors of the Torres Straits wore boar's tusks believing that, by so doing, they acquired the animal's strength and ferocity. More certain in their effect were the fighting bracelets worn by some African people, notably the Shilluk of the White Nile region. Massive rings of ivory were used like a cestus or knuckle-duster to give additional weight to the blow. Metal bracelets armed with projecting spikes were worn by the Masai for the same purpose.

Because of the vast mineral wealth of the continent, metals were in use in Africa much earlier than elsewhere, and much

African jewels. Woman wearing a labret (1) fighting bracelets in metal and ivory (2) gold jewel from West Africa (3)

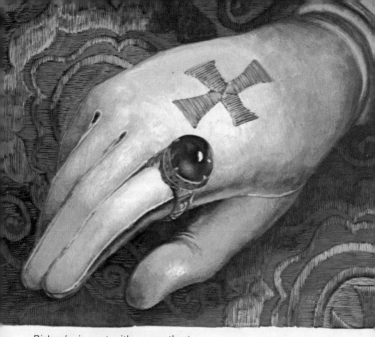

Bishop's ring set with an amethyst

African jewellery is of iron, brass, gold, or silver. On the west coast, jewels were cast in gold by the *cire perdue* (lost wax) process used to make the famous Benin bronze plaques.

Clothes wear out, but jewels last for life; this, perhaps, is the reason for the tight link between a jewel and its owner, but it is not the only one. It does not explain the countless legends of jewels which wax and wane in brilliance according to the state of their owner's health, or the curses that attach to many great stones. Jewels and precious stones probably have more magical properties attached to them than anything else, partly because, by the laws of contagious magic, anything worn close to the body must affect its welfare. Earrings, until quite recently (and perhaps even now), were worn by civilized males to prevent diseases of the eye. Until the time of James I, the sovereign of England annually blessed a number of rings to be worn against the cramp. Today a bishop wears a large ring, usually set with an amethyst, a powerful charm against possible drunkenness at official banquets, or a sapphire, the emblem of chastity.

One particular jewel is closely identified with ancient worship of the great Earth Mother. Simple prehistoric effigies always show her wearing a necklace. *Brisingamen*, which is believed to mean 'fiery necklace', belonged to Freyja, whom modern scholars believe to have been a fertility goddess of ancient Scandinavia. Skialf, Queen of Sweden, who has been identified with Freyja, is said to have strangled her consort Agni with a necklace. This jewel may then have been connected with the ritual killing of the sacred king. Freyja is said to have paid for *Brisingamen* by sleeping with the dwarves who made it on four successive nights. The dwarves who lived in huge caverns under the earth were the magic craftsmen of northern mythology. But there was another mysterious figure, Wayland Smith. Like Haphaestos of the Greek tradition, Wayland was lame. Perhaps a smith was so valuable to the community that he was lamed to prevent his running away. The ivory Franks casket shows Wayland forging the head of his captor's son into a magic jewel.

The Franks casket in ivory, the detail showing Wayland Smith

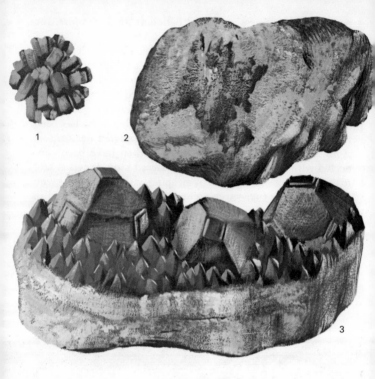

Native gold (1, 2) galena, an ore of silver (3)

GOLD AND SILVER

Gold is the metalworker's ideal medium: he may draw it into
wire as fine as a hair, or beat it into leaf so thin that light will
pass through it. It may be cast to the contours of a thumbprint
or smelted into shot one-fourteenth of a millimetre in diameter.
Pure gold is remarkably stable and impervious to the ordinary
processes of corrosion and decay; a gold coin could lie buried
for a thousand years and yet be found bright as if freshly
minted. The unalloyed metal has a rich soft shine and is waxy
to the touch.

Gold is almost always found in its native metallic state, often in white quartzite rock, or as dust and nuggets in the beds of rivers. Raw gold is seldom pure but mixed with silver, copper or even iron. If the silver content is more than one-fifth it is regarded as another metal, electrum.

Once, *placer*, or alluvial, gold was concentrated by panning. Gold-bearing river gravel was agitated in a shallow pan, the heavier gold being separated by gravity. Sometimes the skin of a newly-killed sheep was anchored to the river bed with stones. Gold dust moving in the current would lodge in the greasy wool. After a time it would be taken out and burned, and the gold washed from the ashes. This could well have given rise to the legend of the Golden Fleece.

Ancient peoples usually refined gold in two stages. In the first, *cupellation*, the gold was heated in a *cupel*, or crucible, with lead. The lead combined with the base-metal impurities and separated as a dross of oxides floating on pure molten gold, or gold and silver alloy. The silver was removed in the second stage of the process by smelting with salt to form silver chloride, which was absorbed by the walls of the crucible.

Although some silver was produced as a by-product of the gold-refining process, most was extracted from galena, a lead silver ore. Sulphur was driven off by roasting, and the resultant litharge converted by reduction into a lead and silver mixture which was separated by cupellation.

Silver is both less malleable and less ductile than gold and also less stable. It corrodes quite readily, especially in a sulphurous atmosphere, and although as much silver as gold jewellery may have been made in the ancient world, all but a few silver pieces have perished.

Before being worked up into jewellery the metal must first be fashioned into sheet or wire, unless, of course, it is to be used for casting. Formerly sheet was made by hammering an ingot to the required thickness. Like many other metals, gold and silver become harder as they are worked, so the process must be interrupted periodically to relieve these stresses by heating to redness and quenching in water. This process is called *annealing*. Modern low-carat gold alloys should not be quenched as too rapid cooling alters their structure, leaving them extremely brittle. Today metals are rolled to uniform thickness between steel rollers.

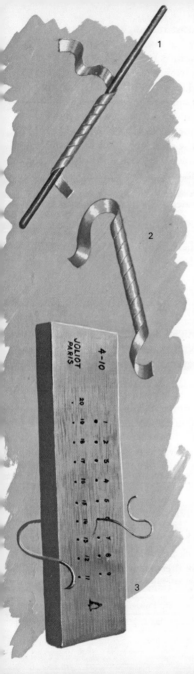

In early times wire was made in various ways. First a sheet was cut into strips. These may have been hammered to round section or rolled between bronze plates. Hollow wire was made by twisting the strip or wrapping it round a mandrel which was afterwards withdrawn. Very thick wire was also known to have been cast. Today the drawplate is used, a thick plate of high-carbon steel punched with a series of holes of diminishing diameters; the wire is dragged through successively smaller holes until it is of the correct gauge. This leaves telltale striations along its length. The drawplate appeared no earlier than late Roman times.

Hard soldering is the method used for assembling the basic parts of a piece of jewellery. Hard soldering em-

Early craftsmen twisted gold strips round a mandrel (1) to make hollow wire (2).

The drawplate, showing a piece of wire being pulled through holes of decreasing diameter

Opposite: gold work ready for soldering

ploys a similar metal to the pieces to be joined, but alloyed to a lower melting point. A flux is needed to help the molten solder to flow and to enable it to wet the two surfaces to be joined. The modern jeweller uses lump borax rubbed down to a milky fluid with water, but the old craftsman probably used cream of tartar prepared from burnt wine lees. Flux was painted onto the joint with a feather, then snippets of solder were laid in place. The job was then brought to red heat on an open charcoal fire assisted by bellows or blowpipe. If all is done well there is a gratifying quicksilver flash and the joint is made. The job is then pickled in acid to remove flux and firescale. A well-married, hard soldered joint is almost invisible. Where several joints have to be made in more than one operation, previous joints are painted with earth to prevent the solder from running out.

Basically there are two ways of producing three-dimensional metal-work: *casting* (little used in ancient work since it used too much metal) and *raising*, or *repoussé*. The sheet of annealed metal is embedded in pitch and the design driven out from the back with suitably shaped punches. Finally the work is reversed and outlines sharpened and detail added from the front. Most sculptural and relief work was, however, produced from dies. The simplest of these were relief carvings in some unyielding material like wood or bronze over which thin gold sheet was pressed or burnished. The results are called *bracteates*. Punches and dies usually of bronze were also widely used. Most objects in the round, such as beads or

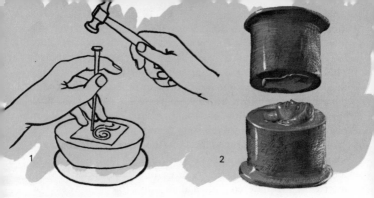

In *repoussé* work the metal is held face down on a bed of pitch and the design hammered out from the back (1). A punch and die (2)

necklace pendants, were made by this method. Both halves of the object were stamped out back and front, then soldered together. The hollow interior was then filled with wax, clay, or magnetite sand to give weight and substance.

The embossed surfaces produced by this method were usually enriched with *filigree* and *granulation*. In filigree work the design was traced in wire soldered to the background. Rarely it was made *à jour*, or open like lace. Granulation used fine gold shot in a like fashion. These were obtained by heating a fragment of gold to melting point when it rolled into a perfectly spherical droplet. In antiquity, and particularly in Etruscan work, grains of dust-like minuteness were massed over large areas to produce a texture of great richness.

Different methods are more suitable for decorating flat metal

A bracteate mould

surfaces. *Chasing* resembles *repoussé*, but the design is struck in from the front, not from the reverse. Decorative punches may be used for a repeated pattern. *Engraving* gives a clean, sensitive line. The pressure of the hand needs to be adjusted exactly to the resistence of the metal. In *tremolo*, or *wrigglework*, the tool is rocked from side to side to leave a controlled zigzag line.

Mercury possesses the curious property of amalgamating with gold without heat, and from Roman times to the present this has been used to gild silver, copper and bronze. An amalgam of mercury and virgin gold was rubbed over the surfaces to be gilded. The job was then heated, driving off the mercury in a vapour and leaving a skin of gold behind. From this comes its name: fire gilding.

To decorate flat surfaces, a craftsman may use an engraving tool (1), which fits snugly into his hand (2). The various kinds of gold decoration include open filigree (3), applied filigree (4), and granulation (5)

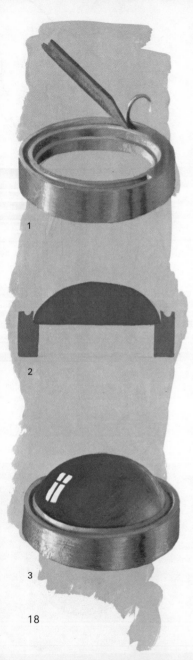

To make a Roman setting, the collet was prepared with an engraving tool (1). The stone was then laid in place (2) and the setting edge hammered over the stone to secure it (3)

Colour is most usually introduced by setting with precious stones. The old goldsmiths used the domed *cabochon* style of cutting in a secure and simple setting. The basic mount was a collet of thin metal fitting closely round the stone. The upstanding edge was thinned down and then burnished over to hold the stone tightly in its place. The Roman setting was often used for ringstones. A seating for the stone was chiselled in the solid metal and then a channel was cut around this. The stone was laid in place and the setting edge driven over it with a punch. The marks of the punch were then gouged away with a round graver.

Enamel was used sparingly but to great effect in some ancient pieces. Enamel is in fact glass, coloured with metallic oxides and fused to the surface which it is to decorate. Several methods of using enamel may be employed. In *cloisonné* the colours are kept separate by

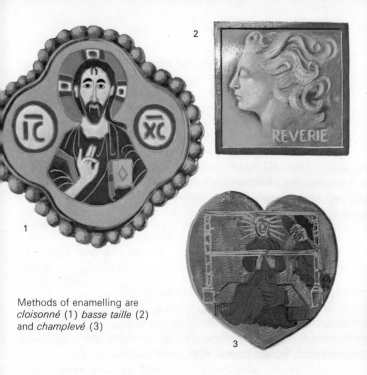

Methods of enamelling are *cloisonné* (1) *basse taille* (2) and *champlevé* (3)

cells of wire or strip. With *champlevé* enamel, the design is carved into the surface and filled with enamel. When an embossed or engraved design is covered with a layer of translucent enamel, this technique is called *basse taille*. When the metal has been prepared for one of these treatments its surface is slightly roughened and then alkalised with saliva. The powdered enamel is packed with a spatula into the spaces prepared for it. The piece is then put to the fire – gently at first to drive off the moisture then fiercely to melt the enamel. This needs great care since many colours are fugitive and have a tendency to disappear if they are overheated. Sometimes, with a large area, the cooling enamel contracts so much as to buckle the metal. The back is often *counter-enamelled* to cancel out this effect. *Niello* is a brilliant black sulphide which is used similarly to enamel, mostly on silver.

THE ANCIENT WORLD

The Early Egyptians

Almost without exception the symbols employed in ancient jewellery are magical or religious in origin. This was especially true in Egypt. The ancient Egyptians treated their dead with great respect and buried them in the jewels they had worn in life, or in cheap copies of them. This surviving evidence shows the Egyptians to have been skilled working jewellers, particularly in the techniques of polychrome inlay. Slips of stone (or glass) are cut into *cloisons* of gold in a rich mosaic-like pattern. This is the technique used to decorate the magnificent pectoral of King Tutankhamun. The vulture symbolises the *ka*, or soul, of King Tutankhamun in whose tomb it was found. Other pectoral ornaments made by Egyptian craftsmen are rectangular in shape and represent a shrine.

Wide and elaborate collars were worn by both sexes, the beads of which were of many kinds. The material was mostly faience, a fused mixture of sand and lime covered with an alkaline glaze, usually blue or green. This material was used for making pendants of many kinds, although hardstones such as lapis lazuli, amazonite, cornelian and amethyst were used as well. Motifs were equally varied. The *djed*, a four-barred column, symbolised strength and endurance. The *udjat*, or eye of Horus, protected the wearer from all harm, especially the evil eye. Horus is also represented by a hawk. Thot, god of learning, is symbolised by the ibis or a baboon.

Scarabs were functional as well as decorative, the reverse carrying the owner's personal seal. Its original is the dung beetle *Scarabaeus sacer*. Patiently rolling across the desert the ball of dung which contained its eggs, this humble insect reminded the Egyptians of the eternal journey of the sun across the heavens. It was the emblem of Kheper, the morning sun god. Scarabs were mounted as rings in a simple and attractive fashion. The ends of the hoop were swaged down very thin and passed through the drill hole, then wrapped round the opposite shoulder.

Tutankhamun's pectoral (1) bead collar (2) five pendants (3) scarab ring showing method of making (4)

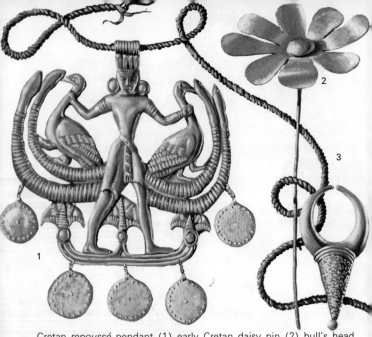

Cretan *repoussé* pendant (1) early Cretan daisy pin (2) bull's head earring (3)

Ancient Greece

Minoan and Mycenaean Jewellery

Minoan civilisation seems to have come to the island of Crete around 2800 BC. Greek legends of the birth of Minos and the love of Pasiphaë confirm that the cult of the white bull was deeply rooted in Bronze-Age Crete, and the bull's head was a common motif in Cretan jewellery.

Minoan culture found its first foothold on the island of Mochlos and in the eastern part of Crete. The daisy pin belongs to this period. Many beads were made of gold, also cornelian, amethyst and crystal. The drum bead is an interesting form based on the fish-vertebra bead of the Stone Age. Around 2000 BC power gravitated to the western part of Crete where it centred on the royal palaces of Knossos, Phaestos and Mallia. The pendant illustrated is in crisp *repoussé* with a flat back, the hollow interior filled with magnetite sand. It was worn hanging from a pin or chain which passed through the tubular top of the headdress.

By the fifteenth century BC, Cretan wealth and power were paralleled by the mainland city state of Mycenae. Here a new and formidable dynasty rose to power, and by 1475 BC, Knossos was in their hands. Early Mycenaean jewellery consisted of diadems with *repoussé* decoration, earrings of the hoop type, discs for sewing to the garments, embossed with butterflies and octopus motifs, and pins and cut-out ornaments decorated with a variety of motifs, deer, cats, naked fertility goddesses with perching doves, and griffins.

The most typical product of the late Mycenaean period is the relief bead. At first these were made of gold, but as metal became scarce glass came into use, at first gilded, later plain. Early relief beads were pierced through the bar-shaped surmount, and the effect when strung would have been that of a fringe. In about 1450 BC, a new form was developed with the beads pierced through the body. These were now strung into denser ornaments. The best designs originated around

Early Mycenaean *repoussé* diadem (1) relief beads (2)

this time, and between 1450 and 1400 BC, granulation and blue enamel were used with exquisite taste. A stylised nautilus is a common motif as are lilies, ivy, rosettes and volutes. Sometimes cult objects are represented, such as jugs, shields and altars.

Although rings with inlaid or plain bezels are known, the most representative carry an intaglio design. The best are cast with the design carved in the solid gold.

Melos and Rhodes

After 800 BC, the Greek lands renewed contact with the Orient. Through Carthage came Egyptian and Assyrian ideas. It has even been suggested that Phoenician master-goldsmiths were at work in the cities of Greece, probably training Greek apprentices. Forms from the submerged Minoan cultures re-appeared. Once more in Crete the goldsmith's craft flourished, and from here sprang the two important schools on Rhodes and Melos.

Typical island earrings are variants of the spiral with elaborated terminals. The elegant earring with griffin's

Earrings from Melos (top, bottom)
Melian rosette (centre)

head terminals, illustrated here, is from Melos. It would have hung from a thin wire passing through the ear lobe. In later types this would have been masked by a rosette. The Assyrian rosette motif illustrated was the usual decoration on diadems of this time. These were either embossed, cut out and applied, or strung on bands of leather or webbing. The other earring shown is a typically Melian design often lavishly decorated with filigree and granulation and elaborated with birds, insects and animal heads.

Fine pectoral ornaments from Rhodes took the form of a band of embossed plaques worn along the top of the dress. The example illustrated shows a winged Artemis figure between two lions. A fringe of pomegranate drops hangs below. Variations on this motif are common, but sphinxes, griffins and *melissai*, or human-headed bees, also occur.

An interesting bracelet design emerged at this time. Formed as a ring broken to admit the wrist and with a beast's head at each terminal, this type is still common in India.

Part of an embossed pectoral ornament from Rhodes

Classical Greek necklaces and three earrings

Classical Greece

The jewellery of classical Greece represents the flower of the goldsmith's craft. Here is dignity without pomposity, fantasy without frivolity. Emphasis, as always in the Mediterranean world, is on the head, neck and shoulders, and earrings, necklaces and diadems are the best represented.

Earrings are mainly a development of earlier styles. The island spiral continues, transformed into a horn shape with an animal or human head at the thick end, the thin end passing through the ear. The W-shaped variant also persists, its proportions now more refined, but it is the boat-shape which is brought to the highest degree of perfection. The latter are often fantastically adorned with pendants on elaborate chains formed as cockle shells and human heads with large rosette-shaped surmounts. These, together with the necklaces, were the most typical creation of the Greek goldsmith. Early classical necklaces were of beads, representing organic motifs

(melons and eggs) with acorn pendants and a calf's head at the centre. Complete examples are rare. The acorn had a special significance as the fruit of the mystical oak which was venerated in the west wherever the tree, with its attendant mistletoe, flourished. In the mature form of necklace, the same motifs recur hanging from a compact band of leaves and flowers, in a delightfully rhythmic composition. Pendants formed as female heads appear to have been a feature of jewellery from the Greek settlements in the Crimea. Rich hoards of gold jewellery were found in this region, where a Greek colony had been established since the sixth century BC.

Filigree gradually supplanted granulation at this time. Gems were rarely used, except in rings, and colour was supplied by touches of *cloisonné* enamel applied with admirable economy. Wreaths were made for ceremonial purposes, and were also buried with the dead. The leaves and berries of the myrtle, sacred to Aphrodite, were a favourite design.

The Hellenistic Period

By the middle of the third century BC, the zestful spirit of Greek civic life had declined. Philip, king of Macedon, hastened to fill the vacuum and before long his nation controlled the Hellenic Federation. When Philip was murdered, his son Alexander was made king at the age of twenty. Within five years he was master of the East, and Greek culture absorbed many alien influences. This was especially noticeable in jewellery, since large amounts of precious stones and metals were released from the treasuries of conquered kings. New techniques were introduced, notably in the inlay of precious stones, and the Heraclian knot motif appeared, probably from Egypt. This potent charm was believed to hasten the healing of wounds. This motif frequently forms the centres of magnificent diadems, often inlaid with garnets and hung with pendants. Another diadem which was to have echoes up to the twentieth century was formed as a band of embossed gold rising to a gable at the centre. An example is illustrated on the opposite page.

The hoops of Hellenistic earrings are frequently threaded with beads of garnet or onyx. The boat type faded out, to be replaced by another style of comparable magnificence. Its basis was a decorated disc from which were hung figures of Eros, winged Victories, amphorae, or the white doves of Aphrodite, perhaps in *dipped enamel*. In this typically Hellenistic technique, molten glass is caught up on a wire and pinched into shape by glass-working methods.

Necklace designs became weaker and more repetitive. A strap of plaited chain supported the pendants, which were usually jars or spearheads. The crescent was an oriental innovation. Richly set with gems it could form the pendant to a necklace of gold beads. Serpents coiled about the wrist or finger as both rings and bracelets. Massive gold finger rings, sometimes with the stone wider than the finger, were equally popular. The jewellery of the Hellenistic period has a rich imperial splendour but the restraint of Classical Greek design is lacking.

Hellenistic diadem with gabled centre (1) two rings (2) diadem (3) with Heraclian knot motif inlaid with a garnet

Fibula with lions (1)
Etruscan disc earring (2)
à baule earring (3)
lentil-shaped bulla (4)
satyr's head bulla (5)

The Etruscans

The Etruscan civilisation flourished in the northern part of the Italian isthmus from about 700 BC until it was eventually absorbed by Rome. Among their Greek and Roman neighbours the Etruscans had a reputation for being cruel and vain. The abundance of jewellery which they have left to us seems to bear out the last accusation. About their skill in handling metals there can be no argument, and Etruscan jewellery reached a height which has never been equalled. Certainly the Etruscan technique of granulation has never been satisfactorily imitated. The problem is to marshal the grains (as small as 180 to the inch) into a pattern and then sweat them in place without the flux boiling up and displacing them, or an excess of solder flooding them. In the 1930s H. P. Littledale discovered how it was done. Coarse filings of high carat gold were mixed with powdered charcoal and heated to melting point in a closed vessel. To solder them in place copper carbonate was mixed with water and fish glue. Heat was applied which converted the adhesive flux into a thin deposit of copper. This amalgamated with gold and made the joint.

Fibulae (clasps) were very popular with the Etruscans. Sometimes these were exceptionally large and decorated with processions of lions. Earrings were of several types. The *à baule* earring took the form of a cylinder, broken to admit the ear lobe, and the ends closed with stylised flowers. The name refers to its resemblance to a bag. Large disc earrings richly decorated with filigree and granulation were also worn, either close to the ear or suspended from it.

The bulla is the most Etruscan of all ornaments. This pendant is typically of lentil shape, or embossed in the form of a satyr's or a lion's head. The lion seems to have been the mascot of ancient Etruria, as it is of modern Florence. Bullae seem to have been made to contain a liquid, possibly scent, since they are hollow and the wedge-like loop from which they are suspended serves as a removable stopper. Bracelets were of several types. The most distinctive was a wide band of embossed decoration bent around the wrist.

Gradually the Etruscans were drawn into the Greek cultural orbit and, as elsewhere in the Mediterranean lands, filigree, the Greek form of decoration, largely replaced granulation.

The Romans

To all intents and purposes, early Roman jewellery is identical with Etruscan in its early and Hellenistic phases. During the austere years of the Republic strict laws forbade its excessive use, but the luxurious mood of the Empire made the vulgar display of precious ornaments a conspicuous target for the contemporary satirist. Petronius makes one of his characters command scales to be brought in during dinner to weigh the ornaments worn by himself and his wife. Martial suggested that the grotesque size of one ring suited it for more convenient wear on the owner's leg. A ring was often worn on each finger. Sometimes several slender rings each set with a single stone were united into one, but more often a single intaglio formed the bezel. The tapered shoulders were often carved, the shank bearing an inscription.

By this time filigree and granulation had virtually disappeared. Roman design called for flat unworked surfaces, and where decoration was needed the chisel provided it. Often the design was pierced right through (à jour) in the technique called *opus interassile*. More than ever the goldsmith's task was to show off a fine stone – Egyptian emeralds polished in their natural hexagonal form, pearls from the Red Sea, and even diamonds, although these remained uncut.

The *crotalia* (rattle) was a typical form of earring, with one stone or pearl supporting three others from a horizontal baton in chandelier fashion. Hemispheres of gold were an Etruscan legacy, sometimes thickly encrusted with emeralds or seed-pearls. Serpent rings and bracelets retained their popularity as did the Heraclian knot. The wheel, however, was a new motif, also from the East. Many bracelets displayed an elaborate centre, a vase, or rosette, perhaps on a broad flexible strap of scrolls or foliage. Sycophantic Roman courtiers would wear a coin bearing the head of the reigning Roman Emperor, seeking favours in return for flattery. These usually hung from loop-in-loop chain with large wheels of *opus interassile* next to the clasp. Another related ornament carried a *repoussé* Medusa-head medallion at the centre of a collar of stout chain. The Etruscan bulla continued to be worn, usually by boys. The Roman crossbow fibula was a cruciform type from the Celtic provinces.

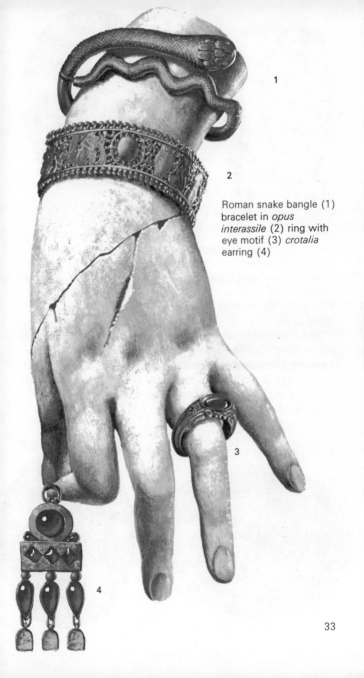

Roman snake bangle (1) bracelet in *opus interassile* (2) ring with eye motif (3) *crotalia* earring (4)

Etruscan engraved gem in blanched agate

Greek engraved gem

Early Engraved Gems

Seals were invented to secure property. The most primitive was a joint of reed which could be rolled across a wad of wet clay to leave a unique imprint. The Babylonian cylinder seal was probably evolved from this and was worn hung from the wrist or neck.

The Egyptians were not the only people to use scarabs; the Phoenicians and Etruscans also carved their gems as beetles. On early Etruscan gems the device or sigil is rendered crudely by juxtaposed drill holes, but in the work of the best period, figures are represented in muscular detail and enclosed in a rope-like border. Hercules is a favourite subject.

Roman gryllus in cornelian (1)
Gnostic engraved gem in jasper (2)

Roman engraved garnet with the head of Jupiter Serapis (1)

Persian cylinder seal (2)
Sassanian engraved onyx (3)

The Greeks were the finest gem engravers of the ancient world and an artist such as Dioscorides enjoyed a status comparable with that of an actor or sculptor. Nevertheless, these artists seldom signed their work and signed gems are generally regarded with great suspicion by the experts. In the nineteenth century, gems were collected with great enthusiasm and many fakes were made by Italian engravers.

Many fantastic designs were used in the Roman period. Some represented *chimerae*, or compounds of several animals, others a comic paradox, like an elephant emerging from a snail shell. Christian gems are rare, but the Alexandrian Greek Gnostic cults produced thousands of an extraordinary character. The most typical represents a figure with the torso and arms of a man grasping a flail and a shield, each leg a serpent, and the head that of a cock.

Great efforts were made to make the subject of a gem agree with the colour of its background. Cows browsed on green jasper. The bearded head of Jupiter Serapis crowned with a corn measure was customarily made in haematite or garnet. Marine deities were made in aquamarine, and the flaying of Marsyas in cornelian. The first cameos were made in Roman times but the art moved to Byzantium after the fall of Rome. Later, intaglios continued to be carved by the Sassanians, the oriental subjects and inscriptions betraying their Persian origin.

NORTHERN EUROPE

The Early Britons

Long before the arrival of the Romans, the British were famous for their skill in working gold and, above all, in enamelling. *Torques*, or neckrings, of tremendous size and weight have been found. A coarse red *champlevé* enamel was used with considerable skill, but gems are unknown. Massive ornaments resembling penannular bracelets with disc terminals have also been found. Some of these are so small that they cannot possibly be bracelets, and since they are equally unsuited for wear as rings it has been suggested that they were dress fastenings.

Three centuries after the birth of Christ began the great tide of migrations which was to sweep away the boundaries of the Roman Empire. Dislodged by the Huns from their settlements on the shores of the Black Sea, the Goths moved on again, westward this time, taking with them the skills they had learned from their Scythian and Sarmatian neighbours.

The Romans left Britain and the Anglo-Saxons came, at first for plunder, then for land – Angles on the uninhabited east coast, Jutes in Kent and the Isle of Wight, Saxons in the west. Roman civilisation, art and learning were engulfed. Only vestigial traces were left of the restrained Provincial Roman style of decoration. In its place came the great beast, an unidentifiable animal, fantastically modified in its journey from southern Russia, and resembling in turn a lion, an elephant, and even a bird. Ornaments were often cast in a technique resembling the chip-carving practised by woodworkers in the remoter parts of Europe until modern times. The materials were bronze, gold and silver. Beads of Baltic amber were strung into necklaces. Beautiful beads were also made of spiralled gold wire and were often combined with pendants set with eccentrically shaped *cabochon* garnets. As always in the blustery lands of northern Europe, the emphasis was on brooches, serviceable fastenings for a heavy cloak or tunic, and of all jewels these are found in the greatest variety.

Ancient British ornaments as they were discovered, and a torque

Brooches

Long Brooches

The prototype of the long brooch resembled a safety-pin in both design and function. Early examples were simple, exploiting the properties of the metal in an ingenious fashion. Although the coiled pin and returned foot were eventually replaced by a fastening more suited to the casting technique, the basic form of the brooch remained. The long brooch was made all over Europe, from Britain to the Black Sea, but each region had its own style. The returned foot suggests that the long brooch evolved separately from the Mediterranean type of fibula, the catch-plate of which was formed in quite a different way. The cruciform shape of the English brooch is very typical and had nothing to do with Christianity. It was cast thin and flat with ample room for embellishment. The decoration is stylised almost out of recognition; only the strangely peering eyes betray its animal nature and show its relationship with the intricate monsters that writhe their way into so much early Northern decoration.

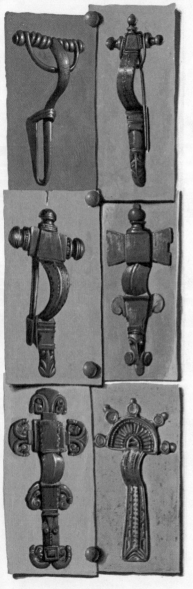

Various types of the European long brooch

38

Saucer Brooches

The saucer brooch divides into two different kinds, the simple saucer brooch and the more complicated applied brooch. The saucer brooch proper is formed as its name suggests but with a rosette of moulded decoration added at its centre. The applied brooch is also round, but flatter, and the decoration takes the form of an embossed and gilded disc cemented to its face. Both occur in the typical zoomorphic style, but also in debased Roman taste which suggests a different parenthood from the long brooch.

The Jutish colonists of Kent used a saucer brooch of a special kind. The one illustrated came from a pagan burial ground at Faversham, England. Of encrusted gold, lit with the dark fires of inlaid garnets, this is a superb example of the exalted craft of *cloisonné* inlay. Almandine garnet has been ground to fit *cloisons*, or cells, of gold strip, the upper edge of which is spread to hold them in place. The bosses are of white organic material which is too decayed to identify. The areas of unset gold are decorated with applied filigree.

Two saucer brooches (1)
a Jutish inlaid brooch (2)

Five pins and three latchets

Ireland

Because of its geography, Ireland had no Roman occupation nor barbarian invasion. Here the native culture took a more natural course. The only alien influence came from the Vikings, and then at a time when the Teutonic style had attained an excellence never reached in England. At the time of the Viking occupation Irish jewels were prized in Scandinavia, and many have been found in Norway.

The Celtic style of decoration is one of whorls and volutes, returns and interlacements – the mathematical adventure of an endless line. The chasing of the latchet is apparently a simple quatrefoil, but its secret complexity compels a second glance. The latchet is a fastening rarely found outside Ireland. The serpentine wire is thrust through the garment, and its curves hold it in place. Its kinship with the pins is obvious. These are called *hand pins* from their resemblance to a clenched fist.

Others are related to that peculiarly Irish jewel, the ring brooch.

The ring brooch was not originally an Irish invention. The practical Romans brought it to Britain at the time of the Claudian occupation, but it had been in widespread use long before that. But it was left to the Irish craftsmen of the eighth century to make of it a great jewel. At the functional level it is a clever device. The pin head has a sliding collar which rides freely round the ring. The pin is stuck through the garment in the usual way. The point is swung up through the gap in the ring which is given a quarter turn, bracing the pin firmly against it by the downward pull of the cloth. In the mature style, which evolved by the middle of the eighth century, the terminals had expanded to fill half of the open centre and had been linked for strength. The brooch was now a complete circle, making it necessary for the pin to be detachable at the head. By this time it was of imposing size and the pin of exaggerated length. The Tara brooch is regarded as the finest of this type so far discovered.

The Tara Brooch

The Vikings

Although it is as shipwrights and woodcarvers that the inhabitants of ancient Scandinavia are best known, their jewellery was made with equal skill. Rich collars and bracelets were worn, the finest lavishly encrusted with filigree and granulation. Others were formed of thick and thin wires combined in a simple twist. Rings for the finger were formed in the same way. Perhaps the most bizarre creations of the Scandinavian goldsmiths were the bracteates. At first the smiths based their efforts on Roman originals, then abandoned them for their native Northern gods, such as Thor riding a goat.

Gotland stands apart from the main Scandinavian land mass. Perhaps this accounts for the distinctive character of the jewels found there. The local variant of the long brooch shows several special characteristics – the square head, the disc on the arch and the elaborate *cloisonné* decoration. An interesting development is shown here – the boar's head brooch. We can trace its growth from the

The development of the Viking boar's head brooch (top to bottom) (1) a drum brooch (2)

primitive wire fibula to a mature form in cast metal with a vigorous chip-carved decoration which subsequently degenerated into a weak pattern of dots or hatching. The saucer brooch too had a distinguished offspring – the box, or drum, brooch. This took the form of a cylinder, the sides sloping in a little. Four decorative pillars were added at the cardinal points, and sometimes the slightly conical roof budded off curious organic motifs.

The tortoise brooch is rare in Gotland, being a Norwegian design. In Norway, the zoomorphic style reached perfection, and the tortoise brooch was its ideal vehicle. Animal motifs branch and weave, extend and interpenetrate beneath the imprisoning latticework. Sometimes, however, a separate motif is framed in each reticulation, and occasionally the framework is absent altogether.

Denmark, too, had its own variation of the long brooch. This was thin and flat with square head and pierced foot, and in its earlier forms crowded with rich decoration.

Bronze tortoise brooch (1) gold bracteate (2) Danish silver long brooch (3) inlaid long brooch from Gotland (4)

A Byzantine mosaic at Ravenna portraying the Empress Theodora

BYZANTIUM

In 330 AD Constantine made Byzantium the capital of his diminished empire. The lives of the Byzantine emperors were encased in a bizarre blend of Christian ritual and oriental pageantry. Jewels reflect attitudes, and one of the mosaics at Ravenna shows the Emperor Justinian and his consort

Theodora encumbered with precious ornaments. Pendants often took the form of a cross engraved with inscriptions or nielloed with the figures of saints. The finest crosses are of *cloisonné* enamels and depict saints and martyrs. The iconoclast movement in the eighth century had an inevitable effect on this type of ornament and was also responsible for the first wave of Byzantine influence which was to transform European jewellery in the Middle Ages.

The Early Christian custom of giving rings as presents probably accounts for the large quantities of rings which have survived. Most were of gold or gilt metal and engraved with religious motifs and inscriptions. Roman *opus interassile* survived in the popular crescent-shaped earrings. A similar type in filigree enamel, granulation and pearls took the form of an inverted arch surmounted by a small medallion.

Byzantium is perhaps more important for its influence on other countries than for the jewels produced in its workshops.

Byzantine cross in *cloisonné* enamel

ROMANESQUE EUROPE

In 800, Charlemagne was crowned Emperor and the Roman tradition was re-imposed on the Frankish lands of Germany and France. The effect of this upon the design of personal ornaments was very marked. The Merovingian love of rich colour survived, but the inlays of garnet and paste were superseded by *cloisonné* enamel and ancient engraved gems. Classical cameos and intaglios were much valued, since it was not until the fifteenth century that western lapidaries were able to practise this exacting technique with real confidence. In the Carolingian period they were mounted in channelled Roman settings, and the pagan subjects were given a Christian interpretation. The tau cross or trefoil brooch appeared at this time, decorated with the acanthus motifs so characteristic of Romanesque applied art. Some earlier forms continued, such as the lobed, circular brooches with bossed centres. Charlemagne did a real disservice to modern scholars by abolishing the custom of burying personal jewellery with the dead.

In 1027 Byzantium and Europe drew even closer with the marriage of the Empress Gisela to Conrad II. A hoard of jewels found in the cellar of a building in Mainz is believed to have been worn at the wedding. The fine eagle fibula illustrated is one of two from this treasure. Typically Byzantine is a pectoral ornament set with *cabochon* and engraved gems pendent from chains and enriched with a filigree lunette.

The characteristic decoration of the period is tightly scrolled Byzantine filigree. Stones and pearls are set in collets with decorative setting edges sometimes rising in light foliated claws. *Cloisonné* enamel in the Byzantine palette of gold, purple and blue imparts to these jewels the placid beauty of an illuminated manuscript. Rather coarse granulation occasionally appears, and loops of metal often outline a border. Probably a course of small pearls, long since perished, was threaded through these. During the Middle Ages, the finest jewellery was made in the workshops of the Rhine and Meuse.

Eagle brooch found at Mainz (1) the Towneley brooch (2)
Carolingian three-lobed brooch (3)

THE MIDDLE AGES

During the thirteenth century the design of jewels underwent a marked change. Byzantine filigree, closely wedded to the surface it decorated, gave way to a new style. The Schaffhausen onyx, a fine Augustan cameo, is set among precious stones in high collets, each tapering to the base and ribbed with four stout claws. The shadowy spaces between are inhabited by heraldic lions and eagles. Unchecked by the concentric borders and regular outlines of the Byzantine style, the design dilates luxuriantly from the centre. During the same period *champlevé* enamel replaced *cloisonné*, and Limoges became the principal centre of manufacture until the sack of that city by the Black Prince. The belt clasp illustrated represents another trend in the jewellery of the early Gothic period, for the sculptural treatment of the figures is quite new.

In the fourteenth century the society that we live in today began to take shape. Power, wealth and costly display were no longer the exclusive privilege of the nobleman, but were also enjoyed by successful businessmen. Jewels, which until then had been made mainly for ecclesiastical and ceremonial purposes, were no longer the symbols of an office or an allegiance, but intensely personal, a manifestation of the ego. Many fell victim to the vicissitudes of fashion and were restyled to satisfy the prevailing taste – another reason for the scarcity of medieval ornaments.

The Gothic architectural style left its mark on jewels as on all the applied arts. Inscriptions were popular and the ring brooch provided a natural vehicle for them. Usually these were of a sentimental nature, but sometimes took the form of a charm. *Basse taille* enamelling was executed with great skill by the master craftsmen of Florence on silver medallions engraved with religious subjects. This technique replaced the *champlevé* enamel of the previous century. An interesting piece of jewellery which emerged at this time was the cap badge worn by pilgrims. These were roughly cast in base metal at all the great shrines of European Christendom and bore the image or emblem of the incumbent saint. With these, pilgrims displayed their piety as others did their wealth, sometimes wearing them all round the brims of their felt hats.

The Schaffhausen onyx (1) ring brooch (2) early Gothic belt clasp (3)

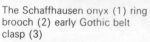

THE FIFTEENTH CENTURY

By the end of the Middle Ages, the dukedom of Burgundy had risen to a position of great wealth and influence, and through the thriving port of Bruges came gold, pearls and precious stones from the Orient to nourish the workshops of the Rhine. Now even the harder stones were not merely polished but cut. The *table cut* in the form of a bevelled rectangle was evolved, and cameo cutting was practised again. Enamelling techniques also foreshadowed the Renaissance a century later. The enamel was applied *en ronde bosse* over scenes and figures modelled in high relief or completely in the round. The hat brooch, a typical jewel of the period, illustrates the combination of enamel *en ronde bosse* with cameo cutting. The portrait is carved in chalcedony, the hat and garments enamelled *en ronde bosse* on a hatched gold ground.

The most typically Burgundian jewel represents a pair of lovers in a leafy bower. The figures were enamelled *en ronde bosse*, the branches fruited small pearls. Occasionally a single figure or a heraldic beast was represented.

Elaborate girdles were fashionable in the fourteenth century. The fabric strap was applied with pierced and embossed metal plaques. Not merely decorative, they were used to support any number of objects including daggers, purses, reliquaries and pomanders. The pomander was characteristic of this malodorous age of growing cities and inadequate sanitation. It took the form of a small sphere, usually of silver, opening into hinged segments like an orange, each labelled with the perfume it contained.

In the later fifteenth century enamel gave way to gold worked in an openwork design of spiky foliage.

Burgundian enamelled brooch set with a ruby, diamond and pearls (1)

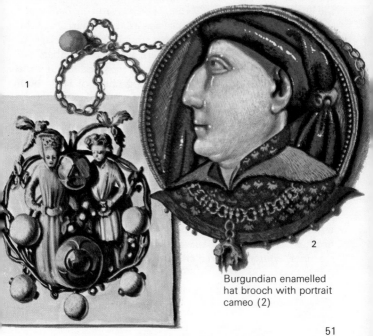

Burgundian enamelled hat brooch with portrait cameo (2)

Orders of Chivalry

The complex social life of the Middle Ages was reflected in the innumerable societies that sprang up at the time – trade guilds, religious associations and jousting societies. The declining status of the knight caused him to flaunt his allegiances by joining one of the orders of chivalry, and princelings strove to enhance their own status by founding such establishments.

Most honoured and exclusive of all was the English Order of the Garter, its membership restricted to 26 including the sovereign. The time and circumstances of its foundation are uncertain, but it is said that a lady dropped her garter in the presence of Edward III and, to silence the comments of the assembly, the gallant monarch fastened it on his own leg with the words 'honi soit qui mal y pense'. Of equally honourable and uncertain antecedents is the English collar of S-shaped links which exists today in the chains of office of the Lord Chief Justice, the Lord Mayor of London and the Chief Heralds. This jewel is believed to have originated in the time of John of Gaunt and various interpretations have been placed on the initial S: *souveignez, soverain,* or *sanctus salvador* are some.

The Order of the Golden Fleece was established in Bruges by Philip the Good, Duke of Burgundy, on his marriage to Princess Isabelle of Portugal. There were 31 members, all *gentilhommes de nom, et d'armes sans reproches*. In 1700 the Emperor Charles V of Austria and King Philip of Spain both laid claim to the order, which then found a home in both countries until the extinction of their respective monarchies.

The Danish Order of the Elephant enjoyed status equal to that of the Golden Fleece. Although one of the oldest of the orders of chivalry, it was reconstituted in 1693, when its number was limited to 30 apart from princes of the royal line. All were to have professed the Protestant faith for 30 years and to have qualified already for admission to the Order of the Dannebrog. According to legend this latter order had a miraculous origin. On the point of defeat in battle by the heathen Estonians, the Danes were rallied by the apparition of a banner, white with a red cross, in the sky.

Order of the Garter (1) Order of the Elephant (2) Order of the Golden Fleece (3)

THE NEW WORLD

There is no way in which we can comprehend the effect that the sights and experiences of a wholly new world had upon the Spanish *conquistadores*, dulled although their perceptions were by 'the disease that only gold could cure'.

Skilled although they were in the working of metals, the native Americans were essentially a stone-age people, and they worked jade, obsidian and agate with extraordinary skill with string saw and bow drill. *Chalchihuitl*, or jade, was sacred, its colour that of growing maize and life-giving water. The Aztec king, Montezuma, entrusted to Cortez a gift of jade for the king of Spain assuring him that each stone was worth two loads of gold.

The ear-plugs and labrets worn in the pierced and distended lobes and lower lip were usually of stone. The ear-plugs were of such paper-thinness and regularity that it seems as if they had been turned on the lathe, but the illustration shows how the

The Maya method of cutting an earplug from jade (from top to bottom)

Obsidian earplugs (1) gold and crystal labret (2)

Maya lapidary made one in jade. The labret was of similar form but seems to have been applied with a medallion of gold.

Aztec cruelty shows itself in the necklaces of skulls carved from shell which were worn in Mexico. Shell jewellery was mostly made in Panama. Magnificent collars of closely strung wedges sliced from the thick shell of the conch, others of sectioned *olivella* shells, and other ornaments carved into frogs, birds and alligators are typical of this region.

From Costa Rica came distinctive jade pendants in the form of an axe head, the top string-sawn into anthropomorphic form. Cylindrical beads up to 15 inches long must have strained the meagre resources of the Indian lapidary to breaking point. These probably supported the breasts of women. Transparent rock crystal was carved into labrets and tubular beads into which a blue feather was introduced, suffusing the stone with a sapphire tint.

It was the emeralds of Colombia which excited the Spaniards'

Shell collar from Panama and jade pendant from Costa Rica

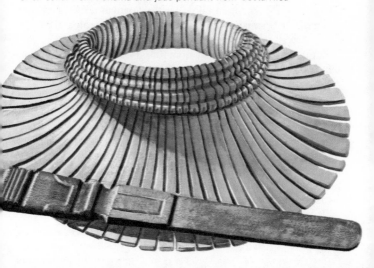

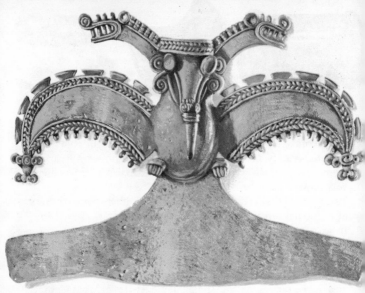

Gold bird pendant from Veraguas, Panama

deepest cupidity. No finer stones had ever been seen. Unfortunately the ignorant assumption that a genuine emerald would resist the blow of a hammer was the basis of their test and hundreds of fine stones must have perished in this brutal fashion. Nevertheless, many found their way to the Old World in the *royal-fifth* share taken by the Spanish crown and they dominated Spanish jewellery right through the colonial period.

Gold, silver, bronze and *tumbaga* were used by the Pre-Columbian goldsmith. Platinum found its way back to Europe in counterfeits of silver coins. *Tumbaga* was gold alloyed with copper to lower its melting point. The surfaces of *tumbaga* ornaments were often enriched by soaking out the copper with acid, leaving a skin of pure gold. The *cire perdue* method so widely used in South America is thought to have originated in Colombia. A wax pattern of the object to be cast was encased in clay, a gate being provided to admit the metal. This mould was baked to harden the clay and drive out the wax. The molten metal was then poured in, and when cool, the finished casting broken out. In this way undercut forms of great intricacy would be perfectly reproduced. The drawback was that breaking the mould made *cire perdue* essentially a process for making single pieces. To reduce weight and economise on metal, a clay core was sometimes included as part of the mould, resulting in a hollow casting. Veraguas, Panama, was noted for cast bird pendants described as eagles by Columbus when he discovered the territory in 1502.

The Peruvian goldsmith was noted for the skill with which he handled sheet metal. The thin metal was usually cut to a regular curved outline embossed with small repeated angular motifs and hung with pendants.

The Peruvians were also skilled at combining gold and silver, plates of the two metals being sweated together and then worked into an ornament. A cockade-like head ornament exists in this style, the pierced base hung with pendants. Crowns and plumes for the head were made much of in Peru. In another type, a wide band of undecorated gold was crested with a tall nodding plume, also in gold.

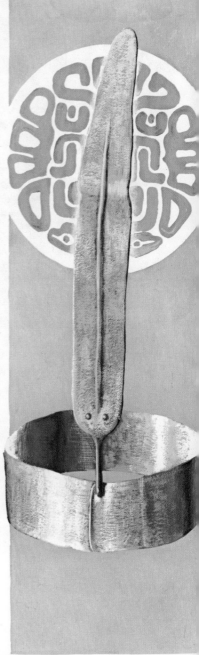

Peruvian head ornament in gold and silver

1

2

3

THE RENAISSANCE

It is perhaps no accident that it should have been in late fifteenth-century Tuscany that man rediscovered the laws of reason that had governed the lives of his Roman and Etruscan ancestors. With this new awareness of his unique place in the universe came a new attitude to dress and adornment. No longer was the female body felt to be the abode of sin to be concealed and inhibited. The elaborate headdresses of medieval times were joyfully abandoned. Now a woman wore her hair like a crown, loosely entwined with strings of pearls and with a jewel hung just below its parting at the centre of the forehead. Loose sleeves and skirts allowed the limbs to move freely and a low neckline made a necklace or pendant essential. No longer were jewels mere accessories of dress but used in dramatic counterpoint to the fluent harmonies of the body. With man's newly won confidence on the seas, precious stones were available in unprecedented quantity and variety, and their strong pure tints were combined in simple groupings.

Ancient cameos were so much in demand that the Italian lapidary was obliged to make them for himself. After the abortive revivals of the Middle Ages, this exacting craft now flourished as it had in ancient Rome more than a thousand years before. With the discovery of perspective these tiny masterpieces, the work mainly of Milanese lapidaries, presented a three-dimensional aspect, and undercutting was used to throw the main figures into relief. This distinguishes them from Roman gems, since the subjects of these more recent pieces were also drawn mainly from classical mythology. It is well known that many Renaissance artists learned the disciplines of their craft at the goldsmith's bench. Domenico Ghirlandaio was so named as a maker of garlands – the jewelled coronals fashionable in his time. Albrecht Dürer was once a goldsmith, and Hans Holbein, although there is no evidence for his ever having been a jeweller, thought sufficiently highly of the craft to produce many excellent working drawings of jewels to be made for his patron Henry VIII.

An early Renaissance woman wearing jewellery; two designs by Albrecht Dürer (1) cameo pendant (2) design by Hans Holbein the Younger (3)

59

Benvenuto Cellini is the best known goldsmith of the Italian Renaissance, but without doubt this is due more to his lively autobiography than to his talents as a craftsman. He was the archetype of Renaissance man, who took his dubious pleasures where he found them and could turn his hand to anything from casting cannon to creating exquisite enamel work. Only one existing piece can be ascribed to Cellini with any certainty, and that not a jewel, but a magnificent salt-cellar commissioned by the king of France. Of even greater value is the detailed manual he compiled, with its precise descriptions of the processes and workshop recipes used by the craftsmen of his time.

Under French royal patronage Cellini and other native designers evolved the style which was to transform Renaissance jewellery in the second quarter of the sixteenth century. These compositions were of scrolls, volutes and strapwork, densely intertwined and richly enamelled. The reverse of every piece is as carefully worked as the front, usually enamelled with the *moresque*, the intricately entwined scrollwork of which, as well as its name, frankly declares its North African origin. Figures were enamelled *en ronde bosse* and lodged in an architectural niche.

Pendants probably represent the finest work of this period. Their three-dimensional character was obtained by making the piece in several parts riveted one on top of the other. *Enseignes* (hat brooches) continued in undiminished popularity. Rings of the time were often set with a single stone in a lobed collet rising to a truncated pyramid between elaborate scrollwork shoulders.

Patterns were produced by a number of designer-engravers and circulated all over Europe. Virgil Solis, Erasmus Hornick and Peter Flötner are some of the best known, but there were many others. These pattern books had such wide currency that it is almost impossible to say where a particular piece was made, since a design which originated in Paris could well have been executed in Nuremberg or Madrid.

Most jewellery at this time was probably made in southern Germany. Successful burghers of these cities had long been noted for their love of display. Heavy gold chains were popular; these were used when travelling, a few links being

German burgher's wife wearing a heavy gold chain

clipped off at a time to pay for board and lodging. Often, too, they supported the whistle which was used to summon domestics. For a long time after the sixteenth century the whistle was an admiral's badge of office.

In spite of the standardising effect of the pattern books, some national characteristics emerged in the jewellery being produced throughout Europe at this time in the workshops of the great craftsmen.

In Spain, pendants were often designed as birds. Parrots from the rain forests of the new colonies were represented, as well as the pelican in its piety. (The pelican is shown opening its breast with its bill to feed its starving young.) These

Spanish enamelled bird pendant (1) Spanish pendant in *verre églomisé* (2)

pendants were of course invariably enamelled and set with precious stones. *Verre églomisé* is a typically Spanish technique in which a scene, generally religious, is painted on the reverse of a glass plaque with black lacquer and brightened with gold leaf. Religious motifs seem to dominate Spanish jewellery. Crosses often show the instruments of the Passion – the nails, scourge, crown of thorns, and so on, used in the crucifixion of Christ. Some religious guilds had a special kind of pendant as their badge. This was commonly of base metal, oblong in shape and inscribed with initials in *champlevé* enamel.

Venice was especially noted for its fine filigree. Strings of light spherical beads were made in this way. *Nefs*, or ship pendants, were also typical of this great trading and seafaring city and these were made out of filigree, or more substantially formed in enamelled gold and precious stones.

Hungary, too, excelled in filigree work, but colour was added with opaque *cloisonné* enamels contained in cells of twisted wire.

In Elizabethan England, courtiers were so lavishly dressed and bejewelled as to cast doubt on the popular image of the sober and reserved Englishman. A man of quality might wear his fortune on his back in a single suit of clothes with a jewel in one ear and a ring on every finger. England and her queen were intoxicated with the victory over the Spanish Armada in 1588 and jewels were made to celebrate this glorious event. These represent the nation as an ark afloat in a sea, calm after the storms of war. Cameos of the queen's head were just as popular. Old Testament subjects were also widely used in English jewellery of the time.

The Spanish mode of dress dominated European fashion until the end of the sixteenth century. Immense ruffs of starched linen framed the face, skirts were expanded by the hooped framework of

Venetian *nef* (1) Hungarian enamelled pendant (2) English 'Armada jewel' (3)

the farthingale, and sleeves, doublets and hose were swollen with padding, or *bombast* – in fact, bombastic is the word that best describes the Spanish fashion of this time.

A similar over-elaboration can be found in the design of contemporary jewellery. From this time, pieces of jewellery were made not only singly but in *parures*. Ornaments for the neck and shoulders were made in suites of three: the *carcanet* (collar) fitting closely to the throat, a matching chain outlining the low neck of the dress, and the *cotière*, a long chain, often with a pendant.

Peculiar to the sixteenth century were those pendants which took the fantastic forms of the legendary inhabitants of the sea: mermaids, tritons, hippocampi and their like, their bodies adapted to match the grotesque shapes taken by the baroque pearl. The Canning jewel, in the Victoria and Albert Museum, London, is a superb example of this type.

The *enseigne* began to fade in significance in the closing years of the sixteenth century, its place being taken by an *aigrette* of curved plumes set with tapered rows of gems. A new

A sixteenth-century woman wearing jewellery; the Canning jewel

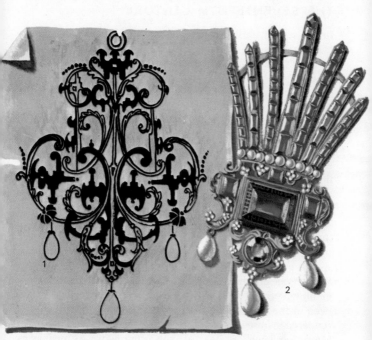

Design by Daniel Mignot (1) cockade
with rows of table-cut stones (2)

attitude to precious stones emerged at this time. They ceased to
be regarded as highlights to the jewel, but were used to trace
out the design in continuous rows. The table cut lent itself
naturally to this treatment. The jewels were characterised
by a new lightness and symmetry and figure work virtually
disappeared. Typical of this new trend were the designs of
Daniel Mignot, published between 1596 and 1616. These took
the form of light formal arrangements of gems against a gold
background. The reverse sides of these beautiful jewels were
intended to be decorated with enamelled designs of a vertical
stalagmitic quality.

This was the time when the diamond assumed the first place
among gems, a position which it has held ever since with few
interruptions and with increasing popularity.

THE SEVENTEENTH CENTURY

In the seventeenth century we see the emphasis drift away from enamels and attach itself firmly to gemstones, especially diamonds. This is not to say that enamelling died out – indeed, several new techniques were developed – but the sculptural quality of sixteenth-century jewellery was not maintained in this century. A jewel ceased to be a self-sufficient work of art, but a complement to the dress. The arrogant inflated styles of the Spanish fashion gave way to a tapered outline. Ruffs now fell gently about the shoulders and skirts were no longer expanded by the hooped farthingale. The dressmaker's use of lighter materials and much lace made new demands on the goldsmith, whose status underwent a change. Now he made only jewels, the fashioning of gold and silver table-plate being left to a separate branch of the trade. This was the beginning of the specialisation which prevails today.

The seventeenth century was marred by disaster. Civil war and plague in England and the protracted agony of the Thirty Years War on the European mainland made death a very imminent reality with which people strove to come to terms, even in the jewels they wore. Skulls, bones and coffins were rendered in obsessive detail, as in the *memento mori* illustrated. Mourning jewellery was all too often worn as necklaces, bracelets and rings, with the name of the deceased traced in gold wire under a slice of crystal in a simple mount. In England, these often bore the cipher of Charles I, CR, who was beheaded in 1649.

In contrast, the gentle craze of tulipomania left a happier impression on the applied arts, and tulips, fritillaries and tiger lilies blossomed on every conceivable kind of jewel. Pea-pods were another favourite motif, holding tapered rows of table-cut diamonds, or rendered in fine *champlevé* enamel.

The Toutin family of Châteaudun added at this time yet another enamelling technique to the jeweller's repertoire. In this, the monochrome background was first fired and the design simply painted on in finely divided enamel colours. The

A woman wearing seventeenth-century dress and jewellery; *memento mori*; flower jewel

Émail en résille sur verre (1) Toutin jewel design (2) rose-diamond cut from the side and top (3)

piece was then returned to the furnace. An enamel of great rarity was the exceptionally tricky *émail en résille sur verre*. The design was engraved in a base of hard glass. The cavities were then lined with gold foil and filled with enamel of low melting point. The problem was to fuse the enamel without cracking or melting the glass – a critical task in those days of charcoal-fired muffles and little or no quantitative means of gauging temperature. This method was practised by a small group of French enamellists for a short time.

As the century advanced precious stones gained in importance. The rose diamond which had been discovered in the early 1600s now took the place of table-cut stones. This style of diamond cutting resembles a hemisphere covered with triangular facets. Cardinal Mazarin is associated with this invention.

The designs of Gilles Legaré are typical of jewel fashions in the second half of the century. *Sévigné* brooches, named after Madame de Sévigné, took the form of a bow balanced with pendent drops. Large *girandole* earrings of a similar form were also worn. *Brandebourgs*, jewelled clasps used to fasten a coat, were at first a male fashion, but were soon taken over by the ladies. With the low decolletage, pearls came into their own. They were also worn as bracelets and earrings.

The seventeenth-century ring had a flat bezel set with a stone or memorial plaque with a toothed border around its setting. The smooth shank swelled at the shoulders and was sometimes decorated all over with a fine tracery of enamel. Inscribed rings were engraved inside the hoop. 'As God decreed so we agreed'; 'This take for my sake'; 'In thee my choice I do rejoice' are the kind of sentiments expressed.

Sévigné brooch design by Gilles Legaré (1) *Brandebourg* brooch (2) seventeenth-century emerald ring (3)

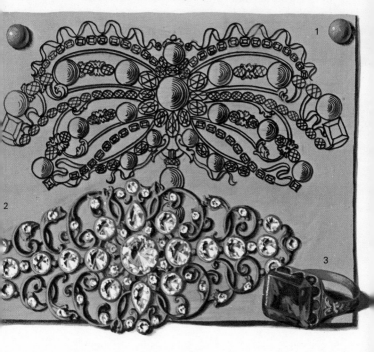

THE EIGHTEENTH CENTURY

To all intents and purposes enamel had disappeared from jewellery by the beginning of the eighteenth century, and even the backs of jewels were in plain metal. This was the age of the diamond. Vincenzo Peruzzi invented the *brilliant cut*, which for the first time fully exploited the unique optical qualities of the stone.

Low necklines called for big brooches, and the *Sévigné* was still popular, together with the similar *girandole* ear pendants. The *crochet*, another very successful style, originated at this time. In this, the complex open decoration of chiselled scrolls and foliage expands to considerable width. The *crochet* was fastened by a strong hook at the back.

Rococo design, which so dominated the other applied arts, made only a brief appearance in jewels in the 1740s. Designs for brooches in this style came mostly from Italy and Spain. Flowers followed in the 1760s, and these styles probably represent the best in eighteenth-century jewel design. Sprigs of marguerite and briar rose were favourite designs for brooches. Technical shortcomings made slavish copying impossible, but the fluent lines of leaf and stem were enchantingly suggested. Sometimes the flowers were combined with ribbons in more formal designs. Linked plaques in this style formed attractive necklaces. These rarely encircled the neck completely, being secured by a bow of ribbon at the nape.

The first really successful imitations of diamonds appeared for the first time in the eighteenth century. Josef Strass was the most celebrated maker of these pastes, which were produced by the addition of lead to flint glass. Rock crystal had long been used to imitate the diamond. In England these stones were called Bristol diamonds after their place of origin.

Shoebuckles occupy a major place in eighteenth-century jewellery. They were worn by men and were often so large as to cover most of the instep. They may have been in silver, diamonds, or the paste already mentioned, although cut steel

A woman in eighteenth-century dress with jewellery; brilliant-cut diamond from the side and top (1) rococo design (2) flower brooch (3)

1

3

was the usual medium. This was an English invention, and Matthew Boulton specialised in its manufacture, producing immense numbers of shoebuckles, snuffboxes, sword-hilts, buttons, and jewellery of all kinds. The metal was cut and polished as a rose diamond would be, and when pavé-set gave a similar effect. Anglomania in France soon carried cut steel over the English Channel and it was manufactured in Paris by Dauffe.

Châtelaines, too, are very much of this century. They were hooked to the costume by a decorated plaque supporting chains from which depended a watch, or *etui*, and a variety of other objects – seal, watch key, writing tablet, etc. Gold was usually employed in their making, while pinchbeck, a yellow alloy named after its inventor, was used at the cheaper end of the trade. Châtelaines were often enamelled or inlaid with agates with consummate skill. The classical style which transformed design in the last quarter of the century demanded engraved stones, and a Scotsman, James Tassie, supplied them, neatly cast in glass. The Wedgwood factory also made cameos in blue and white unglazed porcelain. These were linked into necklaces by fine chains.

Eighteenth-century rings show a great variety of style. Diamonds or garnets were mounted on simple hoops as eternity rings. Half-hoop rings made their appearance at this time. The front of the hoop only was set with diamonds in a single or double row. Most characteristic of the period are those rings set with a single stone or cluster in a cupped setting, engraved on its reverse with a pattern of radiating lines, the shank and shoulders deeply chiselled with scrolls. Royal-blue enamel makes an appearance in late eighteenth-century rings, usually as a background to a closely set diamond motif: a sun in splendour, a cluster, or the sentimental inscriptions and trophies of the age – bows and quivers, musical instruments, hearts, doves and hymeneal torches.

From this time forward, fashion magazines such as the *Journal des Modes* provide a wealth of accurately dated information on the jewellery in current vogue.

Shoe buckles (1, 2) châtelaine with rubies and bloodstones (3) eighteenth-century rings (4–7)

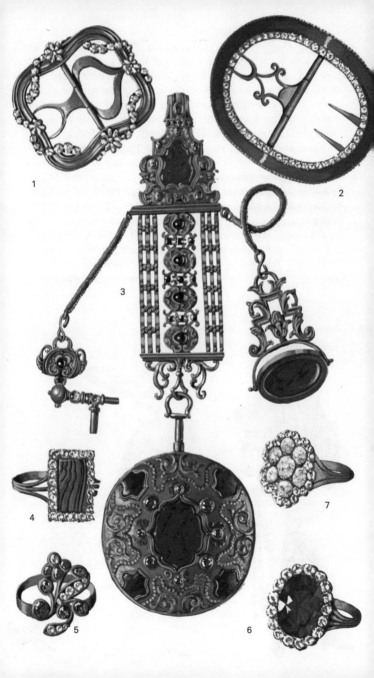

The French Revolution

In 1770 a crime was committed in France which caused political reverberations as profound as the Dreyfus affair. A diamond necklace ordered for Madame du Barry and still uncompleted at the death of her royal protector lay in the vaults of the crown jewellers, Messrs Boehmer and Bassanges. A police officer's wife, the self-styled Countess de la Motte, persuaded them that Marie Antoinette wished to own the necklace and induced the Cardinal de Rohan to act as intermediary. The necklace was handed over, but never reached the queen. She courageously refused to settle the bill of £90,000 and the whole affair was dragged out into the light. La Motte was severely punished, but the Cardinal was found guilty of nothing but incredible stupidity and banished. But for the queen the consequences of the affair lay in the future.

The period of the French Revolution of 1789, when a silver shoebuckle was enough to impeach the owner of being an aristocrat, was no time to be wearing jewellery. Dresses were

Fashions of the French Revolution period

The Empress Josephine wearing
head ornaments

flimsy and economical. Hair was cropped short, and as the
condemned received a similar haircut before going to the
guillotine the style was christened *à la victime*. The *merveil-leuses*, as the fashionable young things of the day were called,
even went so far as to tie a thin red ribbon around their necks.
Short haircuts called for earrings and these were often
fashioned as diminutive guillotines. Rings called *bagues à la
Marat* were in copper set with plaques representing the 'three
martyrs of Liberty', Marat, Chalier and le Pelletier de St
Fargeau. The taking of the Bastille was commemorated in
jewels which carried representations of the former state prison.
Its very stones and iron were converted into rings (*bagues à la
constitution*) or medallions.

Unfortunately much earlier jewellery was swallowed up
by the demands of the national economy. Loyal citizens were
persuaded to give up their gold and silver and were given
jewels of iron or brass instead.

THE NINETEENTH CENTURY

The Early Period

When Napoleon became emperor, fashion responded to the event with imperial magnificence wedded to a kind of bogus classicism. Cameos adorned diadems, stomachers, bracelets and *ceintures*. The key fret was much used, richly traced in pavé-set diamonds. Women wore cameos of the Roman emperors, from Caesar to Constantine, on a collar. Ornaments for the head assumed great importance, combs being worn right on top of the coiffure. These combs were chiefly made in Paris and Rouen, the centres of the jewellery trade. Usually they consisted of a gallery of filigree work surmounted by a row of coral or amber beads. No fashionable young girl would be without two combs, one set with pearls to wear with white, the other with coral to wear with a coloured dress. The ornamental heads of both were interchangeable on a single comb fitting. Combs set with red or green pastes were made in Germany, Italy and Switzerland. Others were set with marcasite or strass.

Tiaras were often very elaborate. A frequently recurring design was of open scrolls pavé-set with diamonds, with pearl drops or emerald briolettes hanging freely in the interstices. A portrait of Caroline, queen of Naples, shows her wearing a tiara in supposedly classical taste; a cameo of Mars forms the centre and a row of graduated pearl drops hangs at each side.

Napoleon's campaign in Egypt ushered in a craze for sphinxes and scarabs and *bagues hiéroglyphiques*. The *collier à la vainqueur* was composed of linked hearts, 20 in number. Coral was at the height of fashion and the *Journal des Modes* for the 8th January, 1807, informs us that it was worn as small beads strung in five or six rows. Amber enjoyed a like popularity. Later in the year this useful publication describes collars of pearls hung with a cross of turquoise, coral or diamonds. Rings designed as clasped hands were for long a peasant tradition in the western part of France, but in 1808 Parisian jewellers copied them, the central motif being carved in coral or malachite.

In 1813 Prussia rose against the French army of occupation. Many Prussian women gave up their jewels in order to finance the campaign and received in return jewels of cast iron suitably inscribed 'Gold gab ich für Eisen' (I gave gold for iron).

A report in the British *Ladies' Magazine* of January 2nd, 1815, serves as a kind of epitaph to French Empire jewellery. The Empress Josephine's jewels had been consigned to an English lapidary for sale. Diadem, tiara, *aigrette*, rings and brooches, including one set with a magnificent sapphire measuring 1 inch by 1½ inches valued at 50,000 guineas, all were to be sold by Eugène Beauharnais to pay off the demands on his mother's estate.

The mood of licence in social relationships which pervaded the years of revolution and war produced its inevitable reactions in taste and manners. In the belief that things would start again where they left off, or perhaps from force of habit, the Bourbons sought to bring the dignity of the *Ancien Régime* back to court.

Jewellery took on the forms of the previous century in the self-conscious 'style Pompadour'. Those of the French crown jewels which remained after a robbery in the previous century had incredibly

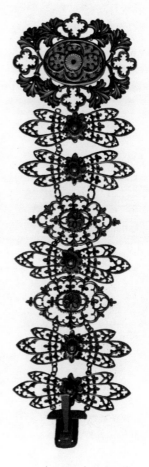

Jewel in Berlin ironwork

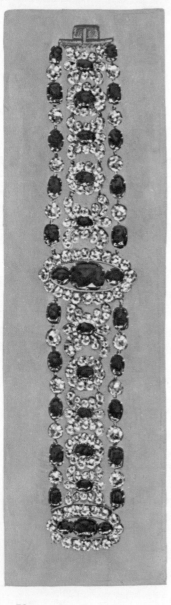

survived these perilous years, part of the time in the hold of a ship anchored off Brest, and were now given to the brothers Bapst, the court jewellers, for remodelling. They were redesigned by Everard and mounted by his brother Frédéric in 1816. One magnificent parure contained some of the celebrated rubies of the royal collection. The beautiful ruby and diamond bracelet illustrated was from this collection.

Nineteenth-century naturalism expressed itself in botanical terms. Improved techniques made it possible for the craftsman to make jewels which copied actual flowers very closely. The style developed over a period that spanned half the century. Diamonds were sometimes supplemented by coloured stones. Some flower jewels of the 1840s were set with turquoises and pearls alone. These, however, were not very successful; it seems that only the tremulous lights of a diamond can convey the essential frailty of a flower.

The blooms were often mounted *tremblant* on a con-

A ruby and diamond bracelet which formed part of the French crown jewels

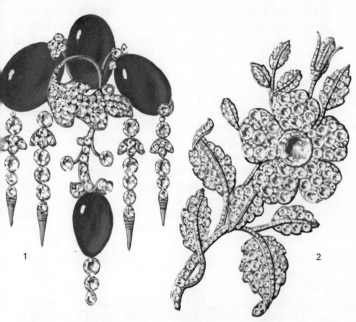

Diamond and carbuncle brooch (1) diamond flower brooch (2)

cealed spring so as to quiver in wear. Slender raceme-like drops gave movement to brooches of the mid-century, often combined with the carbuncles so fashionable at the time. Leaves were occasionally enamelled green around 1845. Lilies, convolvulus, barley ears, lilac, currant and bryony were used in some of the most beautiful jewel designs of the nineteenth century. But above all, wild roses, five sprays of which could be worn as a suite of brooches or as a garland for the head, were the most successful.

It was in England that the early nineteenth-century taste for filigree originated, perhaps acquired from the Indian colonies where it had long been practised by the local craftsmen. No matter what their ancestry these massive parures of necklace, two bracelets, pendent earrings, *girandole* brooch and cross remain in surprising numbers as a tribute to the skill of the goldsmiths of the time. Most of this jewellery is English or

French and seems to have been made between 1820 and 1840. French examples are usually assay-marked with a ram's or eagle's head. A more formal design with a decoration of coloured gold leaves may indicate French work. English pieces are never marked and the design is generally looser. This jewellery is seldom of much intrinsic value and in the saleroom deservedly fetches prices far in excess of its worth in stones and metal. Amethysts, pink topazes and translucent green chrysoprase were combined with half-pearls, emeralds and turquoises, with diamonds to temper the rich harmonies of coloured stones and gold. The filigree settings were highlighted by gold granules centring tight tendril scrolls or arranged in pea-pod fashion. Leaves, flowers and scallop shells stamped from light metal, or touches of red enamel, lend additional interest. Often the collars do not completely encircle the neck and are extended at the back by chains of plump, decorated links. The stones are held in light collets filed into claws and are usually foiled.

Cameos of malachite and shell or the brightly tinted little plaques of glass mosaic from Rome are sometimes set in this way, although the large size and detailed nature of such stones lends them to more simple settings of plain gold connected by festooned chains. Such work is usually of Italian origin. Stones such as bloodstones, eyed agates, amethysts, cairngorms, garnets and topazes, were often mounted in the simplest way possible as pendent earrings and *rivières* (necklaces of a single row of stones).

The cases in which all these jewels are contained may give a very rough idea of their possible origin. English cases were of red leather lined with white satin. Elaborately tooled cases in dark green and black were from the European mainland. But the only really certain proof of origin is an assay mark on the jewel itself.

Rings of this period were often half hoops set with rubies, garnets, emeralds or turquoises in light decorative settings. Two styles bridged the Georgian and Victorian periods. One was the *ferronière*, a pendant resting on the forehead and supported by a chain which encircled the head. The other was the striking, gold longchain which ladies of the time wore around their necks and which reached down to the waist.

Early nineteenth-century
filigree jewellery set with
pink topaz and chrysolite

The Victorian Period

The mood which dominated Victorian England was one of intense enthusiasm. The Victorians were enthusiastic about everything – the colonies, the Crystal Palace, fossils, Him, church brasses, the steam engine, especially the steam engine. Victorian enthusiasm for the machine amounted to infatuation, and to their wondering minds the new manufacturing methods seemed to rival the bounty of nature. Aluminium watches with machine-made chains were advertised in the 1870s. That they should bother to make a watch in this unlovely metal is significant enough, but that 'machine-made' should carry the same cachet that hand-made has today gives a curious insight into the Victorian scale of values. By the 1880s the honeymoon was over, and the intense young people of the Aesthetic movement rejected the machine with as much passion as their parents had embraced it.

An interest in architecture and archaeology was no longer the exclusive field of a few specialists and a widespread interest in history gave rise to a disastrous wave of church restoration. The steam engine led to improved transportation and tourism arrived. Victorians could now indulge their taste for ruins in Italy, Greece and Egypt. All these factors had a powerful influence on the design of nineteenth-century jewellery and led to a wonderful profusion of styles for the collector to study. The machine had an even more dramatic impact on the trade and cheap mass-production methods imposed new disciplines on the designer.

Thanks to Beau Brummell, men no longer wore jewellery of any significance. Shorn of his own splendour, it was up to a man's wife to exhibit his wealth and success by displaying the jewels he had given her. His unmarried daughters were permitted only the simplest jewels.

Jewellery from 1837 to 1860

At the beginning of the Victorian period filigree was replaced by relief designs of scrolls and foliage pressed from light metal – designs more suited to mechanical production methods. Carbuncles looked especially rich in this type of setting but peridots, aquamarines and chrysoprase were also effectively used and large shell cameo brooches were

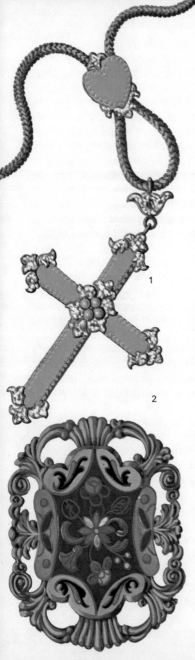

given a similar treatment.

A very distinctive form of enamelling was in use at the time of Queen Victoria's accession, in which simple bouquets of flowers were depicted on a black ground in *champlevé* technique. Often the two techniques were combined in brooches and bracelets. Attractive longchains of slender cartouches in this style occur. In others the links are of tiny enamelled serpents. Scrolls and rosettes in gold are more common patterns for chains, whilst elaborate ropes of patterned links are often secured by a little hand in a lace cuff with a jewelled ring upon the finger. Hands recur frequently in the designs of this period. The *croix à la Jeannette* was a French peasant design which found favour. The cross fleury was of enamel or carbuncles entwined with a diamond serpent and suspended from a heart. Serpent designs of every kind dominated jewellery at this time. Bracelets in this style show surprisingly little variation. The body, beautifully jointed

Early Victorian *croix à la Jeannette* (1) gold and enamel brooch (turned on its side) (2)

and sprung, was either enamelled in translucent royal blue or opaque turquoise and the head was applied with a diamond fern leaf. A necklet was usually of tapered chain forming the body, the head set with a coloured stone, usually a carbuncle, with another in the heart-shaped pendant which hung below the jaws. The heart always has a crystal compartment for hair concealed at the reverse. This was a peculiar feature of jewellery right through Victorian times. From this we also see that hearts were a popular element in early Victorian jewels – used, in addition, as pendants to bracelets of stamped chain links. Ribbon bows enjoyed equal popularity, particularly as the central motif of a gold necklace.

In France in the 1850s ribbon bows dominated a distinct type of necklace combined with elaborate festoons of chain. This jewel was invariably set with rose diamonds and foiled emeralds mounted in silver and gold in the style of the eighteenth century.

The French campaigns in Algeria at this time evoked an interest in the elaborate knots and tassels which were a feature of Moorish dress. These were soon translated into jewels, principally brooches and bracelet centres encrusted with filigree and enlivened with the pallid brilliance of chrysolites and the rich glow of almandine garnets. Other entwined forms, having the same source of inspiration, were plump rings and ovals interlinked and applied with a fern leaf or cluster of grapes and lopped branches of burnished gold twisted around a large garnet, amethyst or citrine.

Early Victorian snake bracelet

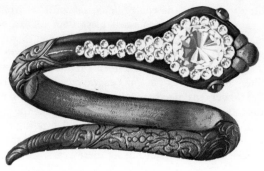

Knot brooch with garnets and pearls

Large pins for the hat or coiffure were usually made in pairs joined by a chain and frequently in Algerian taste – a knot or a simple spiral. Big imitation pearls also formed the heads of these pins but the most successful had pear-shaped heads in royal blue or opaque white enamel enclosed in webs of gold scrollwork. Large cartouche-shaped brooches were made in this enamelling technique, the centre being set with an arrangement of hair on a plaque of opalescent glass. Pavé-set turquoise was also used in many of the other styles mentioned above.

A typical bracelet of the 1850s had a big oval centre and tapered sides. The centre often framed a miniature, the sides being finely made of flexible links engraved with the scrolls, shells and flowers that decorated nearly every flat gold surface at this time. Delicacy obliged Queen Victoria to wear the proud insignia of the Order of the Garter as a bracelet giving rise to the innumerable strap and buckle designs fashionable for rings, bracelets and brooches during these years.

Many rings at this time were set with flower-like clusters of half-pearls with smaller diamonds or coloured stones at their centres, the shoulders being parted and richly chased.

Pendants carved as a Maltese Cross in white chalcedony had centres of coloured golds set with turquoises and other stones. White chalcedony was also used in brooches as a background to a spray of flowers.

Although many of the jewels mentioned on this page were imitated in base metal and paste, the Victorians made jewels of other non-precious materials which were of a far too individual nature to be called costume jewels.

Mrs Brougham of Burslem copied ivory with commercial success in a white porcelain sold under the name of 'Parian'. This was very popular made into brooches and bracelet clasps. Opalescent Belleek porcelain was also moulded into jewellery. Little of this jewellery remains and most is damaged.

The taste for coral persisted into the early Victorian period. As one might expect, it was chiefly worked in the ports where it was landed, particularly Naples and Sicily. Sometimes it was left in its native branch-like state. The pale-pink variety was more often carved into flowers, each leaf and petal being separately worked. The spiral forms of fossil ammonites were

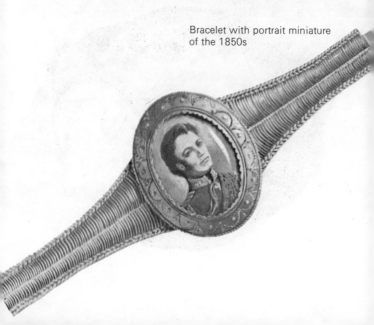

Bracelet with portrait miniature of the 1850s

combined into jewels illustrating the Victorian mania for science and education.

The hair of a deceased friend or relative was not always hidden away at the back of a jewel but fashioned into a jewel itself. Hair was braided into a wide strap as a bracelet or a dense cord as a collar, the mounts being engraved and sometimes set with carbuncles. Unfortunately the mounts are often all that remain today.

A great deal of seed-pearl jewellery of a quite distinct type survives from this time. The designs usually imitated those of more precious jewels and formed extensive parures. A mother-of-pearl base was made and the pearls sewn to it with horse hair. Floral and strap-work designs were common. The dark translucency of tortoiseshell was effectively used in bracelets representing gnarled and rotten branches.

Reference has already been made to the extraordinary reverence in which the Victorians held the things of the past. Until the 1870s the main influence on Victorian taste was

Bracelet of plaited hair, with hair monogram under crystal

Floral seed-pearl jewel

Gothic architecture. Gothic cusps, quatrefoils and mouldings were everywhere in early Victorian jewellery. The style lent itself particularly to machine-pressed gold work, the design often boldly modelled on a matted ground. A few tiaras exist composed of an ungraduated row of pinnacles cut from onyx and set with coloured gold enlivened with minute enamel flowers. Their comparative rarity and similarity suggest that they came from the same workshop. Pugin designed a number of jewels which drew heavily upon architectural motifs. Berlin ironwork, too, adopted the Gothic style. First among all designers in this manner was undoubtedly Froment-Meurice of Paris. His approach was a literary one, his subjects drawn from history rather than the actual jewels of the Middle Ages. Knights, dames, saints and angels act out their parts in a little proscenium of gold tracery.

Although the Gothic style overlaps the middle and late Victorian period, two other schools dominate all other historical styles at this time; Renaissance and classical. Copies of sixteenth-century jewels were produced with great

Pendant by Carlo Giuliano (1)
Gothic tiara (2) brooch by
Froment-Meurice (3)

accuracy by some workshops during the years 1870–1900, and in the 1870s many pendants in the style known as *Holbeinesque* were made. These were of oval form, the centre stone enclosed in a wide enamel border set with coloured stones and with a drop hanging below.

Among the many famous names associated with the nineteenth-century Renaissance style, that of Carlo Giuliano stands apart. Few will deny that the Giuliano family were the greatest goldsmiths and enamellists working in nineteenth-century England. Taking the vocabulary of the Renaissance jeweller they rephrased it into a language that belonged to them and their time alone. Tempted by the whole palette of enamel colours they selected principally black and white to shade scroll-work of a restraint and delicacy that many have imitated but none have equalled. Carlo Giuliano could recognise possibilities in a diamond that most craftsmen would not even accept as of gem quality and devise the perfect setting for it. To him the value of a gem was immaterial; only its colour was important. Besides the Renaissance style Carlo Giuliano also worked in the Greek manner and also evolved a *moresque* necklace composed of several rows of small pearls with mounts of black and white scroll-work. A distinctive feature of his necklaces is a large S-shaped necklace fastening, and his mark CG applied in a small oval plaque.

Undoubtedly it was Greek design that had the greatest influence on Victorian jewels from the 1850s to the end of the century. Besides actual copies made with painstaking exactitude from Greek, Roman and Etruscan models, Greek motifs were borrowed piecemeal and combined successfully with Victorian forms. The circular brooches of the

Enamel Holbeinesque pendant of the 1870s with carbuncle and yellow chrysolites (1) Gothic necklace by John Brogden with rubies and emeralds (2)

1860s provided an ideal vehicle for applied filigree in Greek style. Stone cameos carved with the heads of gods and bacchantes were mounted as brooches in borders of ovolo, anthemion, or key-fret patterns frequently decorated with black or white enamel. Classical ram's heads in gold *repoussé* often accompanied this type of decoration. Necklaces in the form of a strap of Milanese chain fringed with urn-like drops were copied with great success from Hellenistic originals.

Fortunato Pio Castellani, the Roman goldsmith, was first to introduce the classical style. He was particularly successful with Etruscan granulation. Fine though the work of Castellani is, the secret of Etruscan soldering eluded him, and his jewels lack the crispness of the originals. Giuliano also worked in the classical style and a tiara exists of his which is the exact counterpart of a Greek original.

Giacinto Mellillo of Naples worked in the classical Greek style. The pin illustrated is based on a Greek earring although the figure of Eros is

Cameo brooch (1) bracelet by Castellani (2)

in *cire perdue* casting, not, as it would have been in the Greek original, hollow sheet metal. The bird seems to be based on Greek dipped enamel although here again the technique is quite different. Mellillo is also known to have worked in the Renaissance manner. His jewels seem to have been unsigned and were contained in boxes of cedar lined with maroon satin.

Excavations at Nineveh inspired many jewels in the second half of the century. Bracelets in the form of a wide hinged band were decorated with processions of figures, based on Assyrian bas-reliefs. Lotus flowers which were worked into earrings and brooches were also of Assyrian inspiration.

The opening of the Suez Canal in 1869 turned attention towards Egypt and Sarah Bernhardt's success in the play *Cleopatra* in the 1880s started a fashion for Egyptian jewels in turquoises and oxidised silver. Necklaces were made in silver gilt and enamel of papyrus motifs linked into festooned chains caught up at the sides by hawks' heads.

Three pins by Giacinto Mellillo and an Egyptian-style brooch

The spread of railways made the remoter parts of the British Isles accessible to the tourist and local craftsmen hastened to fill the demand for souvenirs. The beaches were combed for agates by visitors who presented them to local jewellers to be cut and mounted. As these pebbles were often unsuitable for cutting, the tradesmen, only too anxious to oblige, substituted Brazilian agates cut in Germany.

Queen Victoria's affection for Balmoral Castle led to a fashion for Scottish jewels. Grouse claws and dirks formed brooches set with cairngorms and amethysts. Simple annular brooches and strap and buckle designs were inlaid with variously coloured agates mostly in silver. Immense cairngorms, amethysts and crystals also were set singly as brooches.

West's of Dublin specialised in jewels from the Celtic past. Large penannular brooches and especially the magnificent Tara brooch were reproduced in silver. Ancient oaks embedded in the peat of the Irish bogs provided excellent material for carving into jewels. The yellowish-green serpentine marble from Connemara was inlaid in silver shamrocks and carved into charms often in the form of a pig.

In 1800, John Carter and Robert Jefferson of Whitby began

Scotch pebble brooch with agates, onyx, cornelian, and a cairngorm

Roman mosaic

Florentine mosaic

carving jewellery from jet. Whitby jet reached a peak of popularity in the fashion for mourning after the death of the Prince Consort in 1861. Fossil marbles from Torquay and the blue john of Derbyshire also provided jewels for the tourist.

On the mainland of Europe, the Italians and the Swiss were the first to realise the attraction that mountains and ruins exercised on the romantic and wealthy traveller. The peasant costumes of the Swiss cantons were represented on enamels painted in a palette dominated by pink and mauve. Sometimes the backs were counter-enamelled with the coat-of-arms and the name of the district.

Roman mosaics were assembled from minute fragments of glass to depict classical ruins in a border of black or red. The mounts drew heavily on classical patterns and were often inscribed 'Roma'. A quite different form of mosaic was made in Florence. Stones, notably malachite, cornelian and white chalcedony, were carved and fitted flush with a black ground making a wide variety of delightful flower and bird designs.

Much of the European peasant jewellery to be seen in British antique shops and auction rooms reached Britain on the backwash of the Grand Tour. The nearness of the French and Belgian Channel ports accounts for the predominance of Norman and Flemish pieces. In the neighbourhood of Rouen the dove of the Saint Esprit is a favourite design but the other districts of Normandy adopt the cross, which is a typical feature of French peasant work. These designs were carried out in sprays of branching scroll-work and set with crystals in large conical collets. Belgian provincial jewels use similar designs and techniques, although the smaller stones are set in rosette-shaped mounts of gold when the background is silver and vice-versa. In the province of Antwerp, a heart surmounted by a crown was the traditional design. Many Dutch jewels are of an extremely bizarre character. Metal spirals protruding from beneath the cap at each temple support a *tremblant* plaque of metal. In the district of Gelderland, women wore a closely fitting gold helmet. Rosette-shaped buttons were worn by men and coral necklaces by women.

Filigree, usually silver, was widely used in European peasant jewellery. The Swiss wore large round filigree brooches, with a bow motif pendent below. In Norway, the *sölje* was the most typical jewel. Of circular form, these brooches may be very large, decorated with filigree or *repoussé* scrolls and hung with the tinkling pendants typical of the western districts. These pendants are of several forms, including saucer-like Maltese crosses or crinkled leaves. Pendants are absent from the *sölje* of the eastern districts, which have a solid, almost Frankish, look.

In the Iberian peninsula jewels vary from village to village. In Portugal, as in Norway, reflecting pendants, often fish-shaped, were combined with filigree. The metal was mostly gold. Pendent earrings were made from a thin plate of gold pierced and engraved with tracery. Long tapered earrings were cast from silver in Spain and set with foiled crystals. At Salamanca garlands were made from massed seed-pearls.

European peasant jewels. Dutch gold headdress from Gelderland (1) silver gilt *sölje* from eastern Norway (2) dove of the St Esprit from Normandy (3) Norman cross jewel (4) Portuguese earring (5)

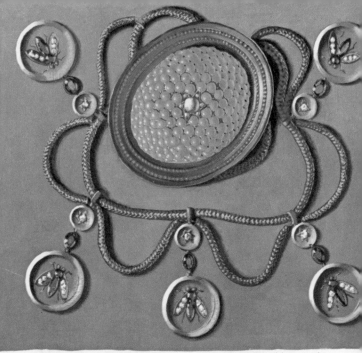

Mid-Victorian fly necklace set with diamonds and peridots, and a brooch pavé-set with turquoises

Jewellery from 1860 to 1880

The unlovely housefly finds a cherished place in mid-Victorian jewellery, particularly on necklaces. With wings glittering with rose diamonds it perches lightly upon a round *cabochon* crystal or carbuncle. Five of these may hang from festoons of Brazilian chain, the snake-like pattern used for key chains, or one may form a simple pendant. Intimate combinations of diamonds and coloured stones or enamels were popular. Faceted amethysts had sprays of seed-pearls or rose diamonds inlaid into their surface. The enamel of the time was of an opaque turquoise colour. Bosses of this were often inlaid with diamond stars and set in borders of half-pearls or thick turbanned gold wire. Turquoise was a fashionable stone of the 1860s. Pavé-set, it formed round or oval bosses which centred all kinds of jewels. Gold was given two new treatments. In one, pickling in acid imparted a sort of bloom. In the other, jewels were pressed into a bowl-like concavity from which the jewelled or enamelled centre rose like a bud. The filigree decoration was reflected in this as though in a trick mirror. In the 1860s and 1870s, dense fringes of tagged drops were suspended from pendants, brooches and earrings.

Two unusual jewels experienced an evanescent popularity. The dress was looped up at the front and sides by the *porte jupe*, a medallion hanging by chains from the waist. Trumpet-shaped holders of crystal and gold were used for the bouquet. The gypsy setting, in which the stone is sunk into the metal surface, forming the centre of an engraved star, was used in rings. Other rings were formed of gold serpents entwined to form a wide band.

A Celtic flavour is discernible in certain buckler-like jewels set with formal arrangements of *cabochon* amethysts and carbuncles and lightly applied with filigree. Hair styles at this time encouraged the wearing of large earrings which took varied and fanciful shapes. Tortoiseshell piqué was suc-

Four mid-Victorian earrings (1–4) four rings (5–8) and jewel set with diamonds, emeralds, and an amethyst (9)

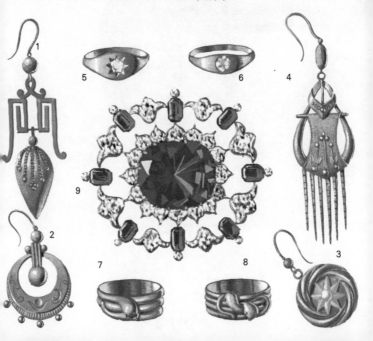

cessfully used in all kinds of jewels, the domed ground of dark shell being inlaid with flowers, stars and tiny studs of gold and silver in simple patterns.

At the close of the nineteenth century, South African discoveries made diamonds more plentiful, and in the more valuable jewels coloured stones recede into the background.

The traditional elements of the trade in England remained curiously impervious to the 'cranky' new philosophy of Art Nouveau. Nevertheless, Art Nouveau scroll-work found its way into every kind of jewel in the 1890s. The new taste for asymmetry also led to a revival of rococo designs. In these the scroll-work outline is traced in pavé-set diamonds on an open trellised ground with a peridot at its centre. A simple but versatile fashion consisted of a suite of five diamond stars which could be worn as tiara, necklace, or brooches. Flower designs were almost as popular. Sprays and the heads of daisies were pavé-set with diamonds or in a cheaper version with half-pearls in gold. Diamond necklaces fringed with

Rococo brooch with peridots and diamonds (1) half-pearl necklace (2)

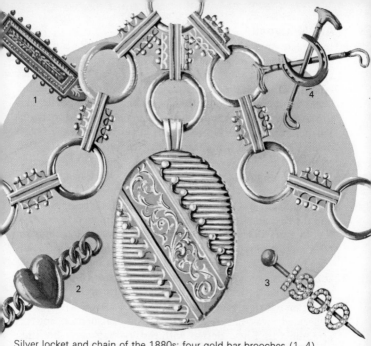

Silver locket and chain of the 1880s; four gold bar brooches (1–4)

icicle pendants counterpointed with husks and blossoms also lent themselves to conversion into tiaras for formal occasions.

Silver jewellery was very popular in the 1880s and many engraved lockets on wide beaded chains and fetter-like bracelets survive in this metal.

Women were now beginning to poach with increasing audacity on the male preserves of politics, the professions and especially sport. This had its effect on jewels as well as dress. Sporting brooches usually took a horizontal form and designs included golf clubs, riding crops and tennis racquets. Other brooches reflect the frivolity of the 1890s and represent wishbones, mistletoe, clover and newly emergent chicks. The newly discovered demantoid garnets of Siberia were used to give a reptilian green to diamond brooches representing frogs and lizards. Dog collars were an essential part of jewellery at this time and appeared either in the form of a broad band of plain velvet or as a circlet of pearls with diamond mounts.

Art Nouveau

In the late nineteenth century, the jewellery trade had begun to suffer from the malaise that was infecting all the industrial arts. The limitations of the mechanical production techniques which had been so passionately acclaimed at the time of the Great Exhibition of 1851 were now making themselves felt and the jeweller's art was in danger of being imprisoned by them. Furthermore the mood had begun to turn against the lavish display of diamonds, and fashion reacted in two ways. One led to the rejection of jewellery altogether, the other to a search for a new language in jewels, the like of which had not been seen since the sixteenth century.

Germinated by the hothouse ideals of the Pre-Raphaelites and the Arts and Crafts movement in England, it was nevertheless in Paris that Art Nouveau was to blossom and flourish. New motifs emerged, exotic, organic, unhindered by threadbare romantic associations. Roses and nightingales there were still, but also sycamore seeds and maribou storks, orchids and disembodied butterfly wings, no longer the objects of sterile imitation but strangely related elements of a larger whole. This, it seemed, was nature blasphemously fragmented and reassembled to a new design with results that were shocking, even sinister, and occasionally of a beauty that makes one catch the breath. Suddenly, at the end of a century that seldom honoured its craftsmen, we read the names Mucha, Lucien Gaillard, Vever, Wolfers, Ashbee, now accorded the recognition usually given to artists in other media.

Perhaps even harder to explain than the extraordinary growth and fecundity of Art Nouveau was its untimely end. In 1903 Gabriel Mourey expressed his fears: 'Its intensity is so great as to be almost alarming. Whither is it tending? Some of its excesses are dangerous; what will be the result?' A journalist in St Petersburg mentioned the predominance of Art Nouveau shop fronts at this time and went on to describe how in the space of a few years almost all were torn out and remade. After a life span of only one generation the movement had drifted like a spent mayfly into the shadows of the Great War. Fortunately we still have the jewels, but they are horrifyingly fragile and need to be handled like fine china.

The iconoclastic character of Art Nouveau philosophy led

to a clean break with contemporary techniques or sometimes a return to older ones. *Plique à jour*, till then the plaything of the Russian jeweller, was used to imitate the cool tints and translucencies of vegetable tissue, the gloss of newly fired enamel softened with a wash of hydrofluoric acid to impart a light bloom to its surface. Carbuncles were too rich for the new palette and turquoise, when used, was cut with a tracery of dark matrix. Now crystal, obsidian and amber bud organically from silver or green-gold settings. The esoteric effects of cats' eyes and alexandrites, of little value at that time, were greatly admired, but the jeweller was not afraid to use diamonds when the design demanded it.

René Lalique was the greatest of Art Nouveau jewellers. His designs show a brilliant dichotomy of almost ruthless daring and sensitivity. Superficially the brooch illustrated represents a dragonfly. A second glance shows us with a shock close to nausea the immense claws that expand on either side and the

Art Nouveau dragonfly brooch by René Lalique

placid siren extruded from the creature's jaws, its eyes forming her headdress, the wings attached to her shoulders. This is no designer's chimera but a seeming paradox of nature, the vibrating spirit of a summer pool, and the savage larva of the winter depths. A similar paradox is seen in other jewels in which tender human forms in carved ivory or moulded glass are framed by brittle plant motifs in rose diamonds and enamel. Lalique was no less adventurous in his search for new materials. Magnificent hair ornaments were carved in horn representing leaves and sycamore seeds and combined with obsidian, crystal and gold. In unchanging materials Lalique strove to express transfiguration and decay: the overblown flower, the winter at the heart of summer. Lalique's work is extravagant and decadent, but evolution itself is endlessly extravagant and decay is an essential element in the biological process.

Vever too worked in the manner of Lalique, but his designs are less impetuous and are characterised by a peculiar delicacy. Sprays of opal blossom, strange spiny fruit bodies, fronds of algae and dandelion clocks, all these motifs were given a delicious dewy freshness by the clever use of rose diamonds. Vever worked the simple rose-diamond loops of his pendants into the composition in a particularly honest and pleasing fashion. Like Lalique he signed his jewels with his surname in block capitals. Vever sometimes designed for the great firm of Boucheron. He is also known to have collaborated with Eugène Grasset whose designs, usually allegorical, were too often spoiled by a rather turgid literary element.

Georges Fouquet and the Czech designer Alphonse Mucha also worked in close partnership. The robust girls with gorgeous hair which made Mucha's posters so appealing were brilliantly interpreted in gold and enamel by Fouquet. After the 1914–18 war Fouquet worked with his son Jean in the geometric style of the 1920s.

The jewels of Joe Descomps possess a naive and perhaps too obvious charm. Enigmatic sphinxes and wistfully smiling girls are typical of his work. His mark includes a spider on its web.

In Holland, Bert Nieuhuis broke completely with both French and English tradition. There is Dutch solidarity in his four-square shapes worked with quatrefoil designs around a

Jewels by Vever (1) Joe Descomps (2) Georges Fouquet (3)

central stone. In Germany too, angular geometric motifs were popular, related to the mainstream of Art Nouveau design only by their originality. The manufacturers of Pforzheim were quick to adopt these tough appealing designs and turned them out in considerable variety. In Germany, Art Nouveau was called *Jugendstil*. Henry van de Velde, although a Belgian, worked in Germany. The exaggerated thicks and thins of his scroll-work have a calligraphic quality unrelated to Belgian Art Nouveau.

In Belgium, Philip Wolfers used the iconography of Lalique to great effect and, although any further comparison would be unfair, his work has a full-blooded theatrical vigour which is very distinctive. Wolfers used elephant ivory from the Belgian Congo in many of his creations. In more than one

pendant its mellow tones are used to depict a tragicomic mask. Female figures modelled with great competence from gold or hardstone are another feature of his work. In his many foliate designs Wolfers contrasted the soft green *plique à jour* enamel with veins of pavé-set rubies. His jewels were signed 'P.W. exemplaire unique' on the reverse.

There can be no doubt as to the British ancestry of Danish design at this time. Eric Magnussen, like most Danes, worked in silver. Belt buckles were his best known creations, pierced from sheet metal in designs of fragmentary scroll-work. Georg Jensen of Copenhagen is the best known of Danish silversmiths. His foliate designs set with stained chalcedony and amber have the robust quality that typifies Danish jewels. Moyens Bollin also made use of vegetable motifs that have the same succulent quality.

C. R. Ashbee founded the Guild of Handicrafts in 1888 and can really be said to have been deeply involved with the Art Nouveau movement

Mask pendant by Philip Wolfers in gold, ivory, opals, and a pearl; *Jugendstil* pendant with diamonds, cornelian, and amethyst

from the very beginning. Peacock designs dominate much of his work and his necklaces make clever use of light festooned chain. The pendant illustrated here incorporates Ashbee's characteristic motif of the peacock.

The cult of the amateur was both the strength and the undoing of British art jewellery at this time and too often the charm of an irregular finish was felt to be a substitute for sound craftsmanship. Of Omar Ramsden, at least, this was far from true. A specialist in the making of church plate, Ramsden made few jewels and these were of a religious character. Drawing heavily on the medieval tradition his jewels also show a strong Art Nouveau influence, as the pendant of St Beatrice shows. It is probably a mistake to identify the Art Nouveau and Arts and Crafts movements too closely. With rather different aims, they tended still to converge at certain points. Henry Wilson, while definitely belonging to the latter, gave to his jewels a heraldic dignity which is quite distinct from Art Nouveau.

Jewels of the *Art Nouveau* period by Georg Jensen (1) Henry Wilson (2) C. R. Ashbee (3) Omar Ramsden (4)

THE TWENTIETH CENTURY

Improved techniques and the use of a stronger metal, platinum, led to a new style in diamond jewels of the Edwardian period. Lighter and almost invisible settings became possible, giving an air of restrained delicacy to these simple designs of garlands and ribbon bows.

The armistice restored contacts with Paris after the war and with the designs of Jean Fouquet. This geometric style was closely related to German *Jugendstil* and was to influence design almost until the outbreak of the Second World War. Its inspiration in the early days of 1925 was purely abstract and designs were built up from oblongs, squares and circles. Sectioned and superimposed slabs of platinum, enamel, pavé-set diamonds and semi-precious stones created interesting chromatic harmonies and contrasts. At the same time the firms of Cartier and Lacloche were developing a style based on the chinoiseries of the eighteenth century.

In the 1930s the strength of the geometric style was vitiated by over-elaboration. The jewel of the period was undoubtedly the diamond double clip; two mitre-shaped clips intended to be worn singly or together as a brooch. These were invariably pavé-set with diamonds or their simulants and the flat surfaces relieved by piercing in a debased geometric style or with simple motifs apparently derived from Moorish architecture. More obviously oriental designs were exploited with greater success by Cartier; in his jewels sapphires and rubies from India were often set among the diamonds. The chain link and buckle motifs of the period lent themselves naturally to bracelets, necklaces and pendent earrings but were also applied to another kind of jewel, the hat brooch. A typical design would be composed of two rings of onyx or frosted crystal flanking a pavé-set diamond centre. The cocktail watch and cocktail ring were closely related, embodying gable, link, half-cylinder and formal scroll motifs in polished gold or platinum usually set with diamonds and calibré-cut rubies. The late 1930s saw a break with the geometric style and a

Edwardian diamond pendant (1) 1920s clip by Jean Fouquet (2) 1930s diamond double clip (3) 1930s hat brooch in onyx, crystal, and diamonds (4) ruby and diamond ring (5)

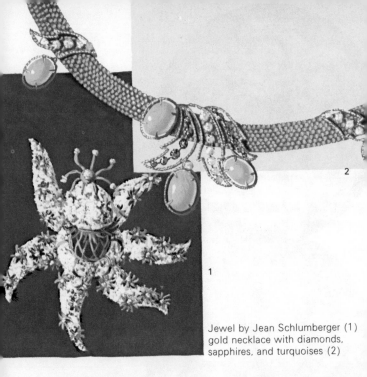

Jewel by Jean Schlumberger (1)
gold necklace with diamonds,
sapphires, and turquoises (2)

return to scroll and floral designs of a rather heavy character.

During World War II, the only innovation of the time was the *minaudière*. An invention of Messrs Van Cleef and Arpels, the *minaudière* was a compartmented case usually in a white alloy named *styptor* containing cigarettes, powder, rouge, lipstick and so on. The fashion did not last long, however, for the practical reasons of weight and bulk. One of Van Cleef's more lasting contributions was a clever technique of mounting gems which made the setting invisible.

After the war, jewel fashions continued the trend towards a greater freedom. Many matching brooches and earclips in coloured gold and rubies were made in stylised flower designs, and necklets of ribbed tubular chain were equally popular. More recently, turban-like designs delineated in corded gold wire and densely set with turquoises, sapphires, rubies and diamonds have been very successful for bracelets, necklets, rings and earrings. At Tiffany's, in New York, the designs of Jean Schlumberger exploit unusual natural forms in gold lavishly set with coloured stones. Unquestionably the most important jeweller on the contemporary scene is Harry Winston, whose personal shrewdness in judging a fine stone approaches the uncanny. Most of the historical stones to come on the market in recent years have found their way into his vaults with the inevitability of a homing pigeon.

Outside the main stream of what, with no intent to disparage, we will call commercial jewellery are those pieces designed by great artists in other media. Alexander Calder's playful creations in brass or silver wire, hammered or simply bent, display a profound understanding of the properties of cold metal. Georges Braque, at the age of 81, designed a series of 133 jewels in close co-operation with their maker Baron Heger de Lowenfeld. The three principal elements of their composition, textured gold, pavé-set diamonds and thin slices of stone are

Brooch by Pablo Picasso (1) Pomodoro gold bracelet (2) brooch by Georges Braque (3) necklace by Alexander Calder (4)

blended into creations which have their own special kind of tranquil beauty. Picasso's jewels are all in gold cast from plaster or terracotta patterns made by the artist himself.

The brothers Pomodoro, although sculptors by background, are equally well known as jewellers and produce somewhat brutal effects by applying molten forms to smooth surfaces. Yves Tanguy, Max Ernst and Jean Cocteau have all designed jewels as exciting and disturbing as their work in other media and Salvador Dali has designed a series of jewels executed by Alemany.

In our own time the designing and making of jewellery has again been raised from an industry into an art. Never before perhaps have design and making, form and medium been so closely interlocked. Now ideas are drawn not only from the world of organic nature but from the whole world of visual and tactual experience. Pencil shavings, crystal formations, even crumpled bus-tickets have led the designer into a new

Jewels by Andrew Grima. Gold, amethyst, and diamond brooch (1) earrings in black opals, emeralds, sapphires, and diamonds (2)

dimension. Reaction against the bland machine-finished surfaces that encompass twentieth-century life has turned the emphasis to texture as well as form, creating jewels that are not only beautiful to see but that one instinctively reaches out to touch.

Highly individual though the work of the English jeweller Andrew Grima is, the enormous diversity and unvarying high standard of his firm's output make it difficult to select a few examples that are more typical than the others. The designs of Grima himself have a casual, apparently random, asymmetry that in fact masks an unerring sense of balance. Many of these jewels are very large but the light, open designs and broken outlines dispel any feeling of massiveness. Settings of stones are almost invisible, so perfectly are they integrated into the textured gold of the mounts. Platinum, incidentally, is seldom used in these jewels and the majority of this work is in 18-carat gold. Carved emeralds, sapphires, citrines, rubies and amethysts from India give rich effects to Grima's jewels. Grima uses a casting only when the job cannot be done in any other way and this applies to his *objets trouvés*. Acorns, pine needles, leaves and bark are beautifully reproduced in a technique that can best be described as *cire perdue* casting without the wax, for the object itself is used to make the mould and is afterwards burned away to leave a cavity. Pressure is needed to force the molten metal into the capillary-like recesses of these moulds and this is supplied by a centrifuge. Pine needles may be woven into a simple ideograph, and the wrinkled surface of a peperomia leaf set with a single diamond.

The designs of Geoffrey Turk offer a complete contrast. Crisp and disciplined, they are more closely related to continental European trends.

Natural gem crystals, untouched by the lapidary, are a special feature of contemporary jewellery, especially that of Hooper Bolton of London. Topaz, tourmaline, aquamarine and more exotic minerals such as azurite and rhodochrosite are held in settings of great freedom and originality. Casting is freely used and plain surfaces lightly frosted by fusing to them lemel or filings of precious metal.

In Scandinavia, there has been no revival as dramatic as that seen in Britain. In 1904 the firm of Georg Jensen opened in

Copenhagen and they have been making fine jewellery and silverware ever since. Nana Ditzel has designed many fine jewels for this firm. Her calm powerful forms are sometimes counterpointed by a note of restrained tension, like the little stud placed disturbingly off-centre at the front of the bracelet illustrated. Henning Koppel was trained as a sculptor, and his jewels show exciting combinations of violent curves. Soren Georg Jensen, one of the founder's sons, employs simple geometrical forms with considerable success. Much of Eric Herlow's work is in 18-carat gold and rings and bracelets in this metal are set with uncut crystals of quartz gems in light cantilevered mounts.

Sigurd Persson of Stockholm is a significant figure in contemporary jewellery. Unashamedly large and magnificently wearable, his designs show a bewildering variety from mono-lithic simplicity to sparkling lightness. The simple jewels of Inga Britt Dahlquist and Olov Barve are designed around the intriguing forms of local fossils.

Elsewhere in Europe the modern revival has been met with exciting encouragement. Gubelin of Lucerne employs open grid-like designs of lightly contrasted horizontal and vertical elements set with diamonds and coloured stones. Gilbert Albert of Geneva has sensed the possibilities inherent in the curious forms of *tektites*, fragments of meteoric glass, and worked them into his designs. The painter Jean Lurçat worked closely with Albert in the making of a series of mask-like jewels produced in a limited edition by the Swiss watch firm of Patek-Phillippe.

In Germany, the work of Elizabeth Treskow is especially notable and Friedrich Becker's designs show a happy union between the crafts of goldsmith and lapidary. Here also there has been an attempt to revive the ancient Mediterranean craft of granulation.

In the United States, Mary Kretzinger has been very suc-cessful in her use of *cloisonné* enamel and John Paul Miller reproduces complex animal forms with applied textures.

Bracelet by Nana Ditzel (1) bracelet by Eric Herlow (2) enamelled jewel by Mary Kretzinger (3) mask jewel by Jean Lurçat (4) rings by Sigurd Persson (5, 6) ring by Friedrich Becker (7) necklace by Henning Koppel (8)

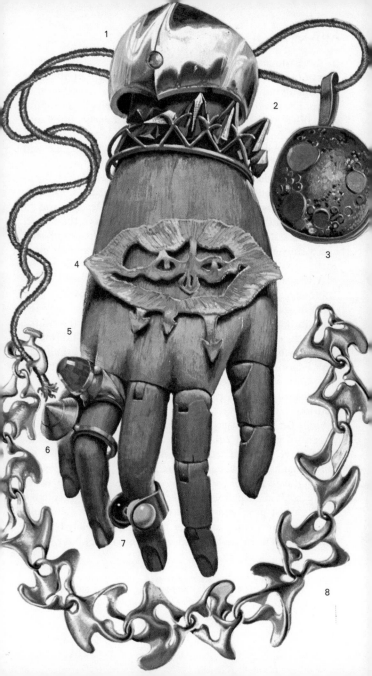

ORIENTAL JEWELS

In the East, more than anywhere else, jewels are a part of everyday life and in India they were often made by itinerant craftsmen who carried the tools of their trade from house to house. The jewels of Jaipur were made of a shell of almost pure gold filled with lacquer, set with gems on the front and enamelled at the back with doves, peacocks, lotus flowers and pinks in a palette of white, lavender, dark-green, blue and glowing red.

Every visible part of the body carried its jewel. The *bazuband* was a plaque bound by silk tassels to a man's upper arm and was set with a configuration of nine different gems of magical significance. The *sarpesh* was tied around the turban and worn with a magnificent jewelled plume. The thumb ring had a sinister dual purpose – to protect the archer's thumb when shooting with the bow and to gain a purchase on the bowstring used to garotte a condemned man.

Women's jewels were of even greater complexity – a crescent-shaped *chand bina* for the forehead, a jewelled chrysanthemum for the hair, a precious stone in the nostril and, in the ears, heavy pendants formed as bells or fish. Hollow ankle-bracelets were filled with shot so as to hiss rhythmically with a dancer's movements, and a ring was often worn on each toe. *Kara* bracelets terminated in the confronted heads of strange birds, tigers or elephants, their gaping mouths grasping a curious fruit.

From Delhi came jewels of mutton-fat jade inlaid with a tracery of gold and ruby leafage. Cuttack was noted for its fine filigree. Another technique of a local character is the so-called enamel of Pertubghur. Here hunting scenes are pierced and engraved in thin gold and fused into the surface of a slice of green glass. Nepalese jewellery is in high-relief depicting the Buddhist pantheon in gold or copper gilt, set with lapis lazuli and turquoise, and it is more closely related to the jewellery of Tibet than to its other influential neighbour, India.

Pertubghur enamel (1) Nepalese earrings (2, 3) miniature of an Indian woman at her toilette (4) archer's ring (5) Persian enamelled earrings (6, 7) Jaipur pendant showing front (8) and back (9)

MINERALS AND THE FORMATION OF GEMS

Most precious stones are minerals formed in the earth under conditions of immense heat and pressure. Some are carried in solution: water will dissolve almost anything if its temperature and pressure are great enough. When this 'mother liquor' cools, crystals are formed. Minerals may also solidify from a molten state.

Sometimes an existing rock is broken down into its constituents by heat. These regroup on cooling to form quite different minerals. If the cooling process is gradual large crystals are formed, sometimes weighing several tons. The huge crystals of beryl illustrated are an example. The opposite is true of cryptocrystalline gems like jadeite, agate and turquoise, which are formed of sub-microscopic crystals closely interlocked.

Usually the ingredients of more than one mineral are present when the gem is formed. These may crystallise separately, as in lapis lazuli which is composed of several minerals existing side by side in a sort of mosaic. Very often one crystal forms inside another as an *inclusion*, sometimes with spectacular effect: rutilated quartz is rock crystal shot through with golden shafts of rutile. Garnet may be included within diamond, zircon within sapphire. Cat's eyes are translucent stones which owe their fascination to the silvery band of reflected light which moves across them. This *chatoyancy* is caused by fibrous crystals or hollow channels, closely massed and orientated like the grain in wood. These reflect the light like a reel of silk, with similar visual effect. When the fibres are arranged in more than one direction, the effect is multiplied into a star. This *asterism*, as it is called, is most commonly seen in ruby and sapphire.

Occasionally the crystal forms in thin sheets like plywood. When light passes from one layer into another of different optical character, *schiller*, the strange vanishing light seen in a moonstone, is the result.

Perhaps the most important property of a gemstone is its colour or, in the case of a diamond, lack of it. This is usually caused by minute traces of pigment present as an impurity, so that one species of mineral can occur in several different

Beryl crystal, with man for comparison of size

colours. Ruby and sapphire are both varieties of the same mineral, corundum, but pigmented with different oxides. When no colouring agent is present we have white sapphire. A few minerals owe their colour to an element which is an integral part of the crystal structure. Without the copper which gives it its characteristic colour, turquoise, for example, would not be turquoise.

But it is not true that all gems are crystalline – opal, for example, is a jelly, and obsidian is a natural glass. Others are formed not in the earth, but in the sea, and among these are coral, pearl and amber, and to complicate matters even further both coral and pearl are crystalline in structure.

CLASSIFICATION AND IDENTIFICATION

Sometimes more than one crystal of the same species attempt to occupy the same space so that they grow into one another. This phenomenon, known as *twinning*, occurs in three different ways. *Interpenetrant twins* grow into one another, producing crosses or stars. *Contact twins* have two crystals united so that one is the mirror image of the other. *Lamellar twinning* causes the *schiller* of a moonstone.

Crystals are classified, according to their symmetry, into seven systems: cubic, tetragonal, orthorhombic, monoclinic, triclinic, hexagonal and trigonal. All possess the property of bending a ray of light, or *refraction*. In gems other than those crystallising in the cubic system, the refracted light is split into two rays. Such stones are classified as *anisotropic* whilst the singly refracting gems of the cubic system (garnet, spinel and diamond) are termed *isotropic*. Non-crystalline gems like opal are also singly refracting. A peridot, zircon, or tourmaline, when examined through the top facet of the stone, will show the edges of the back facets in duplicate. Most doubly refracting stones are *dichroic*, so that each of the two rays is differently coloured by selective absorption. The dichroscope, a cheap and compact instrument, is used to determine this characteristic. A simple dichroscope is illustrated.

There are wide differences in the densities of various stones. These are most accurately established by a specific-gravity test using a chemical balance. A more rough-and-ready test employs methylene iodide and other heavy liquids diluted to known specific gravities. If a stone floats its density is lower than that of the liquid, if it sinks it is higher. Many gemstones possess the property of cleavage, or splitting in one or more clearly defined planes. Topaz and diamond are both examples.

Hardness is of importance to the gemmologist, and the Austrian gemmologist, Mohs, devised a standard scale in which ten minerals are arranged in order of hardness, thus: 1 talc, 2 gipsum, 3 calcite, 4 fluorite, 5 apatite, 6 feldspar, 7 quartz, 8 topaz, 9 corundum, 10 diamond. Conveniently mounted splinters of these minerals are used to determine hardness, but even an ordinary file, of hardness 6, is useful in distinguishing glass from crystal or jade from bowenite.

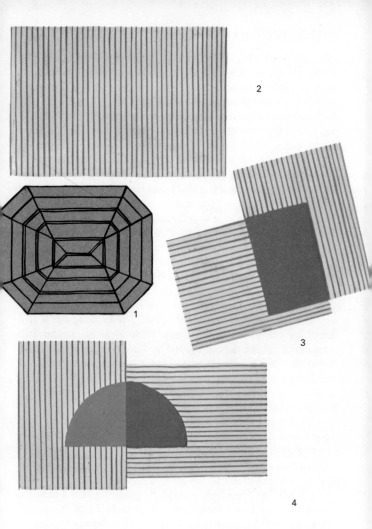

Stone seen through the table showing the edges of the back facets in duplicate (1). A simple dichroscope: a sheet of polaroid showing direction of polarization (2) two halves of sheet should be positioned so that, if overlapped, light will not pass through (3) correctly positioned sheets placed over a stone showing two colours separated by the junction line (4)

CUTS, WEIGHTS AND VALUES

The lapidary cuts coloured stones on a copper wheel charged with a sludge of carborundum and water or impregnated with diamond dust. His equipment has changed little in hundreds of years. Power is supplied with a handcrank which is quite sufficient and gives the lapidary a more intimate contact with his stone. Successively finer grits are used, the final brilliant finish being obtained with tripoli on a tin lap. The gem is cemented to a stick, or *dop*. The angles of the facets are regulated by resting the tail of the dop in one of many holes bored in a vertical post secured beside the wheel and called the *jamb peg*.

The *brilliant cut* was first developed for the diamond, for in this way the stone could be cut with a minimum loss of weight while making the most of its unique optical properties. Most of the light entering the stone is thus reflected by the back facets. The top of a faceted stone is called the *crown*, the bottom, the *pavilion*, and the edge where the two meet, the *girdle*. The larger facet on top of the stone is called the *table*, and the apex of the pavilion, the *culet*. The brilliant cut is also used for many coloured stones, including the zircon and demantoid garnet. A boat-shaped brilliant is called a *navette*, or *marquise*, and a pear-shaped stone may be referred to as a *pendeloque*.

The *rose cut* has already been described; the drop-shaped variant of this is called a *briolette*.

The *step cut*, or *trap cut* has simple parallel facets on both crown and pavilion. This is also called the *emerald cut* as it is usually employed on this stone.

Many stones, particularly sapphires, are given a brilliant-cut crown and step-cut pavilion. This hybrid style is called mixed cutting. The oriental lapidary generally cuts a stone to preserve weight and such stones often have a lumpy appearance. In western countries, however, the lapidary may be willing to sacrifice the odd half-carat in order to improve the colour of a stone.

Even the simple, domed *cabochon* has more than one form. A *tallow topped*, or flat, *cabochon* is used for opals. Star stones and cat's eyes are cut high with a convex back. Carbuncles are often cut with a hollow back to thin down the colour.

The *carat* is the unit used for weighing gemstones. Originally the seeds of a leguminous plant were used as weights. Until recently the carat had a different weight in each of the principal cities, but it has now been standardised at one-fifth of a metric gramme, subdivided into 100 *points*. The *grain* equals $\frac{1}{4}$ of a metric carat and is used for weighing pearls. Precious metals are weighed in troy ounces. Twenty penny-weights equal one troy ounce.

Of the emerald, ruby and diamond it is hard to say which is the most valuable since all three are judged by totally different criteria, but with important stones, emerald and ruby probably compete for first place, with diamond a close runner up.

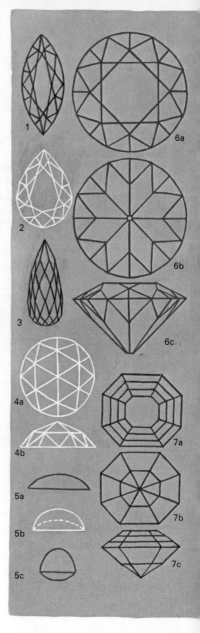

Types of cut. Marquise or navette (1) pear-shape or pendeloque (2) briolette (3) rose cut (top, 4a) (side, 4b) tallow-topped cabochon (side, 5a) high cabochon (side, 5b) double cabochon (side, 5c) brilliant cut (top, 6a) (bottom, 6b) (side, 6c) step cut (top, 7a) (bottom, 7b) (side, 7c)

PRECIOUS STONES

Gems and Magic

For a gemstone, beauty alone is not enough: rarity and durability are equally essential properties. Sphalerite is a stone whose brilliance approaches that of the diamond, but it is too soft to be of value. A fine garnet may be more pleasing than a bad ruby, but whereas the common garnet would be priced in shillings the ruby would be valued at hundreds of pounds. In former times there was yet another consideration. The value and permanence of gems, and above all their vivid essential colours seemed to charge them with supernatural potency. Therefore the sanguine garnet was a cure for melancholia, sky-blue turquoise prevented falling, and rock crystal stopped bleeding. Most magical of all were those stones said to have been taken from the bodies of animals: bezoar from a deer, chelidonius from swallows, draconites from the head of a living dragon. Toadstone was probably the tooth of a species of ray. Large prices were paid for such stones, but where they came from is doubtful.

For medieval man, magic and science were one. Many lapidaries were written by learned men to list the powers and properties of precious stones. The potency of a gem was reinforced by the engraving of the appropriate sigil upon it. A mermaid carved upon a pale sapphire conferred the gift of invisibility. A bird cut in pyrites was of more doubtful advantage for 'having this upon thy right hand thou shalt be invited to every feast and those present shall not eat but gaze upon thee'. The charm was further strengthened by mounting it in the appropriate metal when the right star was in the ascendant.

Today it is difficult for us to understand how these beliefs persisted for so long and gathered so many legends around them. That a carbuncle shone in the dark or that other stones sweated in the presence of poison would, one might think, be refuted by simple experiment and observation, but the link between a cause and its effect were only dimly understood, and the eye of faith supplied many deficiencies. The magical significance of gems has already been referred to in the chapter *Primitive Jewels* at the beginning of this book.

Rough diamond in blue ground matrix (1) diagram showing the
formation of a contact twin (2)

Diamond

The diamond can truly be said to have the most of everything.
Its rarity is legendary; it is the hardest substance known; and
for refraction, dispersion and lustre it has no equal. There are
many gaps in our knowledge of the diamond. We know that
it is crystalline carbon, but we do not know how it is formed.
Its most characteristic crystal form is the octahedron, or the
contact twins known as *macles*.

Most diamonds come from South Africa, where they occur
scattered through immense vertical columns of *blue ground*
extending deep into the earth. Blue ground is a soft, dark rock
which has been extruded when molten through a blowhole in
the earth's crust, but whether the diamonds were formed deep
underground, and were borne upwards, or whether they
crystallised *in situ* is not known. Sometimes the diamonds

Arcot diamond (1) Shah diamond (2) Orloff diamond (3)

weather out and are swept away by rivers, perhaps far out to sea, as in south-west Africa. Stones are also found in Borneo, Brazil, Guyana, Australia and India.

Diamonds fall into three categories, each of which reaches a different market. Industrial stones are of low grade, useless as jewels, but invaluable in industry for wire-drawing, machine tools, rock drills and many other purposes. The value of such material can be as little as £1 per carat.

A blue white diamond is of a pure hard white, lit with a faint blue fluorescence. Too much blue, and the stone is over-blue or 'paraffiney'. Commercial white is still a good colour. Other classes of stones are tinged with *cape* (yellow) or brown. According to the amount of colour present they are classified as: top silver cape, silver cape, light cape, hard cape, or: top light brown, light brown, brown, cinnamon, in descending order of merit.

Fancy-coloured diamonds reach another, highly specialised market and can be of almost any colour. A canary stone is of a clear bright yellow and keenly sought after. Olive and aquamarine coloured stones also occur and pink stones command very high prices. Sapphire-blue stones are even rarer and one could spend a lifetime in the trade and never see a red stone of any consequence. An old fraudulent trick is to make a cape stone appear white with a wash of indigo, and in recent years many low-grade stones have been temporarily lifted into the fancy category by exposing them to radiation, turning them yellow, blue, or green.

A diamond-cutter uses different techniques from the lapidary. His is a trade apart, drawing on the skill of several specialists. First the stone is *cleaved*, or split, to convenient size, then *bruted*, or abraded into rough shape against another diamond, and finally faceted on a cast iron wheel with diamond dust.

Diamonds have been synthesised, but not on a commercial basis since it is cheaper to mine for them. None of the diamonds made so far have been any larger than the size of a pinhead.

Legendary Diamonds

Few things can have been big enough to excite the cupidity of an emperor, but diamonds were certainly one of them. As bribes or booty, reparation or dowry, the really big diamonds are as inextricably involved with history as a royal mistress. It is impossible to exaggerate the bond that existed between a stone and its owner, especially in the East. The Piggot diamond was given to Lord Piggot by an Indian prince. Subsequently it is said to have belonged to Napoleon's mother. Its last owner was Ali Pasha, ruler of Albania, who bought it for £30,000. In 1822 Ali Pasha quarrelled bitterly with his master, the Sultan of Turkey. Fighting broke out in the palace itself. Mortally wounded Ali Pasha summoned his aide and commanded him to destroy the stone before his eyes.

The Shah diamond is an Indian stone weighing 88.70 carats. It bears three inscriptions: one is the name of the prince who first owned it in the Mohammedan year 1000 (1591); the second is dated 1641 and identifies the stone as one of the treasures of the Shah Jehan, builder of the Taj Mahal. The stone is believed to have been suspended by a golden thread from the canopy of the peacock throne. The diamond probably passed into Persian hands in the sack of Delhi in 1739, for the last inscription shows that the stone was in the possession of the Shah of Persia in 1824. Five years later, following the surrender of the rich Khanates of Erivan and Nakhchivan to the tsar of Russia, the Russian ambassador was murdered by a Teheran mob. Fearing reprisals, the panic-stricken Persian government despatched the stone to the tsar in reparation.

The Arcot diamonds are a pair of finely matched drop-shaped stones. They formed part of the Deccan booty and were given to the Nabob of Arcot in 1771. The Marquis of Westminster acquired them for £11,000 in 1837. In 1959 they were sold at Sotheby's, in London, for exactly ten times that amount to Harry Winston of New York.

The Orloff diamond, a rose-cut stone weighing 199.60 carats is said to have been stolen from the eye of an idol standing in a Brahmin temple near Trichinopoly. In 1774 the diamond appeared for sale in Amsterdam where it was bought by Prince Orloff, a lapsed favourite of the Tsarina Catherine, in the vain hope of winning back her regard with a magnificent gift. The diamond was accepted and mounted in the imperial sceptre, but Orloff's relations with the Empress did not improve.

The Koh-i-Noor diamond is part of the British crown jewels. Like so many historic stones, this magnificent gem is very probably from Golconda, India. Its history has been traced back to the year 1304 at which time it was part of the treasure of the Rajahs of Malwa. Subsequently it is believed to have been set in the peacock throne of Shah Jehan. In 1739 the stone fell into the hands of Nadir Shah at the sack of Delhi. It is he who is believed to have given the stone its name: 'koh-i-noor' (mountain of light) is said to have been his delighted exclamation upon first setting eyes on the stone. After his death the stone returned to India and formed part of the indemnity yielded to the East India Company after the fighting in the Punjab. The Koh-i-Noor was presented to Queen Victoria, who had it recut in 1862 to a shallow brilliant of 108.93 carats.

The Regent or Pitt diamond was found in 1701 by a slave working in the Partial mines in India. In order to escape with the stone, the slave wounded himself in the thigh and hid it under the bandage. In return for the diamond, a sailor promised to help him flee but murdered him on board ship. The gem was sold to the governor of the fortress of St George for £1,000. It was later acquired by Thomas Pitt (grandfather of William Pitt, Earl of Chatham) when he was governor of Madras, for the sum of £20,000. The Duke of Orleans, regent of France, bought it in 1717. Together with the Hope and

Sancy diamonds, the Regent was stolen in 1792 and vanished for several years. It came to light in an attic in Paris and was held as surety against a loan which is said to have been of great assistance to Napoleon after he had assumed the dictatorship as first consul in 1799. The stone is now in the Louvre in Paris. It weighs 140.5 carats.

Weighing 3,106 carats in the rough, the Cullinan is the largest diamond ever found, and there is evidence which shows that it may well have formed only part of an even larger stone. Sir Thomas Cullinan, after whom the stone was named, was chairman of the Premier Mining Company in the Transvaal, South Africa. The Transvaal government bought the stone for £150,000 as a 66th-birthday present for King Edward VII. It was cut by Asscher of Amsterdam into over 100 stones totalling 1,063 carats, over 65 per cent of the stone by weight having been lost in the cutting process. The nine principal stones are either in the British crown jewels or in the personal possession of the British royal family.

It is, of course, the fate of a diamond to be recut as fashion and technology develops. J. B. Tavernier, the great diamond merchant of the seventeenth century saw a stone at Golconda and described it as follows: 'It was the biggest I ever saw in my life in a merchant's hands. It was valued at 500,000 rupees, or 750,000 livres of our money. I offered 400,000 rupees but could not have it'. This was the Great Table Diamond. From Tavernier's illustration it appears to have been a long and flat slab-like stone. Its weight, according to him, was $242\frac{5}{16}$ carats. Since that time the stone has disappeared without trace and it is quite likely to have been recut.

Tavernier was more successful in his negotiations for a blue diamond of 112.50 carats in the rough. When cut, the stone weighed 67.50 carats and was set in the French regalia. During the Revolution it was stolen with the rest of the French crown jewels and was never recovered, although it has been suggested that it is identical with the reputedly unlucky Hope diamond.

A diamond was believed to fortify the owner's courage, and also to sweat in the presence of poison. Powdered diamond itself was used as a poison. Benvenuto Cellini would never have lived to record the incident had not the apothecary hired to kill him substituted valueless beryl for the diamond.

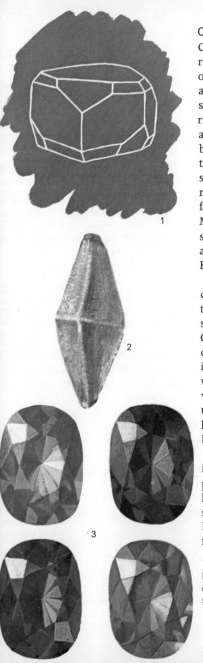

Corundum

Corundum includes both the ruby and the sapphire. All other colour variants but red, and these are many, are called sapphire, with the appropriate colour prefix. The point at which a pink sapphire becomes a ruby is of more than academic importance, since the ruby is by far the more valuable stone. The finest rubies are mined in Mogok, Burma, and the sapphires from this locality are second only to those of Kashmir.

Good rubies and sapphires come from Ceylon, although the colour of these stones is sometimes a little thin. Many Ceylon sapphires change colour from blue to purple in artificial light, a feature which detracts from their value. The colour of most rubies improves in electric light, and it is advisable to buy a ruby in the daytime.

Siam rubies are of a brownish-red colour due to the presence of iron, and much lower in value than Burma stones. All other rubies glow brightly under the Chelsea filter and show strong dichro-

Ruby crystal (1) sapphire crystal (2) four cut sapphires showing the colour range (3) ism, while Siam rubies do not. So-called reconstructed rubies have been made by melting small, commercially useless chips of ruby together with a colouring agent. The joints between the pieces from which the stone is made stand out clearly under a lens. These stones are rare.

Synthetic rubies and sapphires are made in enormous quantities by the Verneuil process, not only for the jewel trade, but for industry as well. Luckily there are some visual differences which a good lens will pick out. In synthetic stones, the colour is distributed in curved zones, whereas in a natural stone this zoning occurs in straight or acutely elbowed bands. Bubbles are usually present in a synthetic stone, with dust-like clouds of unfused alumina. In a natural stone, inclusions are crystalline.

Natural corundum forms in hexagonal crystals, while sapphires are spindle-shaped and rubies form flat crystals.

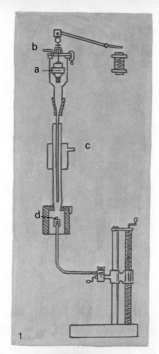

Verneuil furnace (1): powdered alumina and colouring agent are trickled from a box (a) through the intense heat of burning oxygen (inlet at b) and hydrogen (inlet at c) to form a pear-shaped ruby *boule* (d); two synthetic sapphire inclusions (2)

Beryl

Emerald, aquamarine, morganite, heliodore and goshenite are all varieties of beryl. All crystallise in hexagonal prisms. Emerald, by far the most precious, is, at its best, a vivid grass-green owing to traces of chromium. An emerald without flaws is a great rarity, and cracks and fissures are almost always present. The finest emeralds come from the mines of Muzo and Chivor, in Colombia. In 1830, emeralds were found by a Siberian charcoal-burner embedded in the roots of a fallen tree. Subsequently stones of fine colour were found, although they were often much flawed. Emeralds are also to be found in southern Africa, in Heubachthal, Austria, and in ancient times were extensively mined in Egypt. It is likely that Nero's

Emerald crystal as it is found in matrix (1) cut beryl (2) aquamarine (3) morganite (4) heliodore (5)

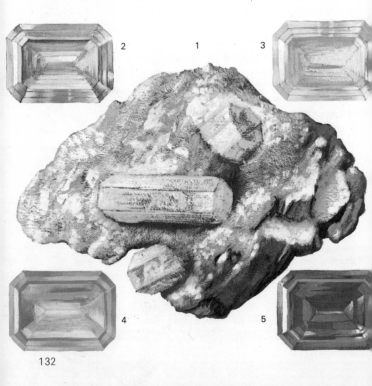

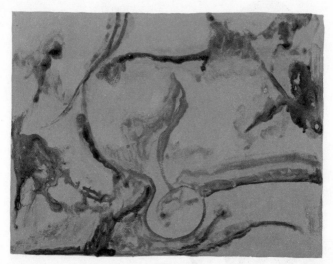

Inclusions in synthetic emerald

famous emerald eye-glass originated from the latter source.

Emeralds are now synthesised by a secret process. This almost certainly involves an autoclave, a hermetically sealed chamber in which vast heat and pressure can be generated. The inclusions in a synthetic emerald have a distinctive, veil-like quality. Nearly all emeralds, including synthetics, turn bright red under the Chelsea filter. A *soudé* emerald is made of two layers of quartz or low-grade beryl stuck together with green gelatine. This deception is surprisingly effective, but the composite nature of the stone becomes apparent if it is viewed from the side in a dish of water.

Aquamarine is generally much clearer than emerald, although 'rain', shining needle-like crystals, is a common defect. The best material comes from Brazil. Other sources are: South West Africa, Madagascar, Siberia, and the mountains of Mourne, Northern Ireland. Aquamarine appears green under the Chelsea filter, whereas pale-blue synthetic spinel, its com-monest simulant, shows pink. Morganite, a pink beryl, is sometimes encountered, but golden-yellow heliodore is most rare. Goshenite is an uninteresting water-white variety.

Chrysoberyl

Alexandrite, a form of chrysoberyl, is a great rarity. It owes its name to the fact that it was discovered in the Ural Mountains on the tsar's birthday. In daylight its colour is a sober green, by lamplight it turns columbine red. It was once popular among patriotic Russian ladies because these were the colours of Imperial Russia. Today alexandrite commands very high prices, especially on the American market. Green chrysoberyl occurs without the colour change. Pale yellow stones are most common, particularly in Victorian jewellery, and are incorrectly called chrysolite in the trade. Chrysoberyl cat's-eye, or cymophane, is admired almost as much as the alexandrite. It is heavier than quartz cat's eye which is a coarser looking stone. Also it is harder: $8\frac{1}{2}$.

Most of today's chrysoberyl comes from Ceylon. It often occurs as interpenetrant twins resembling a slice of pineapple. Purplish synthetic sapphires have often been passed off as alexandrites.

Chrysoberyl cat's eye (1) alexandrite by day (2) and by night (3) 'chrysolite' (4)

Spinel

This singly refracting stone is found in almost every colour. Its hardness is 8 and it always occurs as an octahedron. The most valuable stones are those of a clear bright red. Octahedral inclusions are often present. Red spinels fluoresce under the Chelsea filter. The most celebrated occurrence is in the ruby mines of Badakshan in central Asia. Spinel is also synthesised by the Verneuil furnace process.

Topaz

Besides the typical sherry-coloured topazes, colourless and pale-blue to green stones are common. Pink, or *fired*, topaz is simply yellow topaz which has been heated. The best stones come from Brazil. Other localities yield good yellow material, but the colour may fade on exposure to light. Tiny, clear-white crystals occur at St Michael's Mount, Cornwall. Topaz polishes to a high finish, giving the characteristic soapy feel which distinguishes it from citrine. The hardness of topaz is 8.

Spinel crystal (1) with five stones showing range of colours (2–6) topaz crystal in matrix (7) with blue (8), pink (9) and yellow (10) cut stones

Rough turquoise and
Persian intaglio

Turquoise

Turquoises originally came from Khorasan in Persia, but
were exported through Turkey, hence the name. Stones from
Persia were often enriched with carved and gilded inscriptions
and then cemented to straws for ease of inspection and shipped
to the fair of Nijni Novgorod for sale. In order to put the colour
of a turquoise to the test ancient writers recommend us to
compare it with the blue of a summer sky. When exposed to
grease a turquoise will dull to an ugly cabbage colour. One
should never wash with a turquoise ring upon the finger.

No stone has been imitated with more success – in glass,
porcelain, and chemical composition. Nowadays real turquoise
dust is bonded together with synthetic resin. The colour of
pale turquoise may be improved by dipping in blue wax, and
in past years certain stones were shipped from Persia packed
in moist earth, only to lose their colour on exposure to the
atmosphere. Greenish turquoise is found in the United States.

Odontolite is the fossil bone of prehistoric beasts naturally
stained with mineral salts. The organic grain of odontolite
distinguishes it from turquoise. Turquoise is rather too soft
to be used satisfactorily in the form of a ringstone.

Peridot

This attractive gemstone is found on the island of Zeberged in the Red Sea, and occurs most often in shades of cool lettuce-green. Doubling of the back facets is appreciable, but dichroism is weak. It registers a hardness of between $6\frac{1}{2}$ to 7.

Tourmaline

Beautiful, grooved, pencil-like crystals are typical of this gem. Double refraction is strong, and dichroism apparent even to the unaided eye. Most tourmaline used in jewellery is either dark-green or pink, but practically any shade is possible.

Peridot crystal in matrix (1) and cut peridot (2); tourmaline crystals, including two particoloured stones (3); four cut tourmalines (4–7)

Occasionally two, or even more, colours occur in one crystal. Cat's eyes, too, are not unusual. Tourmaline is found all over the world, but the best stones come from Brazil. In South America bishops wear it in their episcopal rings, in place of the amethyst, and Chinese carvings are executed in pink tourmaline. Pink topaz may be mistaken for tourmaline of the same colour. Tourmaline, however, has much stronger dichroism and double refraction. It is also softer – 7.

Zircon

The jacinth and hyacinth of the Ancients, zircon occurs in all colours. The brilliance and lustre of the jargoon, or white zircon, have cast it in the role of a diamond substitute, but the abnormally high double refraction and consequent doubling of the back facets make its identification a very easy matter. The facet edges may also be very rubbed, as this gem, although of hardness $7\frac{1}{2}$, is very brittle. Red to brown stones are very common, as is a pleasing golden variety which often shows a curious rippled effect under the lens. Brown stones have been fired to produce jargoons for centuries, but bright blue stones are an innovation resulting from the heat treatment of Siamese stones. These occasionally revert to their original colour if exposed to strong sunlight.

Zircon is minutely radioactive, and every stone is undergoing a process of alteration which takes millions of years to complete. Ultimately every zircon is destined to turn green and increase in density before becoming dull and opaque. However there is about as much danger of radiation poisoning from a zircon as there is from a luminous wrist watch.

Feldspar

Moonstone is the best known variety of this species. The sheen, or *schiller*, is due to lamellar twinning, and was believed by the Ancients to increase with the waxing of the moon. Most moonstone comes from Ceylon. Sunstone is a clear gem spangled with highly reflecting flakes of haematite, and much of it comes from Norway. Labradorite is a grey stone

Zircon crystal (1) five cut zircon stones (2–6) moonstone (7) amazonite (8) sunstone (9) labradorite (10)

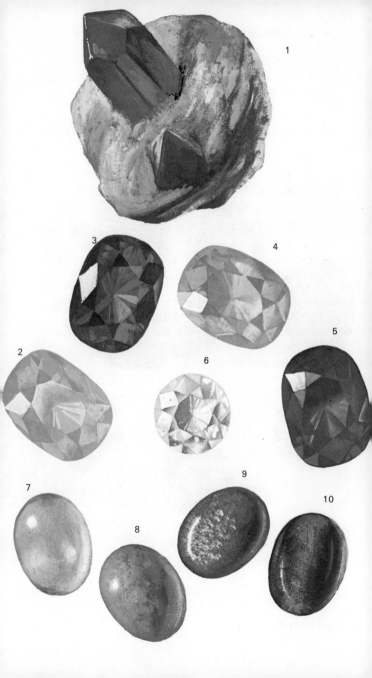

which flashes red, gold, green, or peacock-blue when the light is from the right direction. Obviously it comes from Labrador, where it is often found in the sea as large, tide-rolled blocks. Amazonite is of a brilliant opaque green. The feldspars range in hardness from 6 to $6\frac{1}{2}$.

Garnet crystal (1) and four cut stones: cabochon-cut carbuncle (2) rose-cut pyrope (3) cinnamon stone (4) demantoid garnet (5)

Garnet

The word *garnet* is derived from an earlier form which refers to a fancied resemblance to the seeds of the pomegranate. Apart from the beautiful formation of the crystal, the chemical formation of garnet is also of great interest. Garnets are oxides of aluminium combined with other metals in varying proportions – calcium, iron, magnesium, etc. Almandine is an oxide of iron and aluminium with some magnesium replacing the iron. If the magnesium predominates over the iron it becomes pyrope garnet. There are numerous intermediate states, each with different properties. This is called isomorphous replacement, as the form of the crystal remains unchanged. All garnets are singly refracting. Almandine garnet is purplish-red and when cut as a hollow *cabochon* is called carbuncle, when it sometimes shows a four-rayed star or cat's eye. This stone has a dark steely lustre due to its comparatively high refraction. Pyrope garnet is blood-red and usually faceted. In the London Museum, there is an eyebath carved from a single large garnet, which presupposes a legendary medicinal property. Noah, according to Jewish legend, illuminated the ark with a carbuncle.

Hessonite garnet, or cinnamon stone, shares with zircon the ancient name of jacinth. It is of a rich brown, and under the lens presents a granular appearance, due to the inclusions with which it is filled. Grossular garnet is a green translucent stone from South Africa, often speckled with black like a bird's egg. This stone is rather misleadingly marketed under the name Transvaal jade.

Demantoid garnet was first discovered around 1860 in the garnet gravels of the Bobrovska stream in the Ural Mountains. Its colour is a rich, yellowish-green lit with brilliant dispersion. Asbestos inclusions like tufts of blond hair are nearly always present. The value of these stones is naturally much higher than that of any other garnet. Mostly they are small in size, and anything over a carat is unusual. Unfortunately demantoid garnet is too soft to be ideal as a ringstone, but its unique beauty outweighs this practical consideration. Topazolite is a yellow variety of the same stone. Melanite is a black garnet rarely seen in jewellery. Other forms of garnet include andradite, spessartine and uvarovite.

Quartz

Perhaps most of the stones used in jewellery belong to this group. Rock crystal, or silex, is the basis of them all. This has often been used as a substitute for diamonds and today is often faceted as beads. When containing needle-like crystals of rutile it is called Venus hair stone, or less imaginatively, rutilated quartz, and when the inclusions are of black actinolite, Thetis hair stone. Green aventurine quartz is often cut as beads in India, its place of origin.

The best amethyst comes from Siberia. Its royal purple turns red in artificial light. There are many other sources of amethyst, but the richest, as in all the quartz gems, are Brazil and Uruguay. Citrine, often called topaz by jewellers, is found in Scotland where it is called cairngorm. It is often produced by the heat treatment of pale amethysts. Smoky quartz, or morion, is of a dark molasses colour.

Chalcedony is the cryptocrystalline version of quartz. Agates include any chalcedony that shows a pattern, usually of bands or circles. Often porous stones of uninteresting colour are soaked in dye to bring out the pattern.

Onyx is a black stone often banded with white. It had the reputation of causing bad dreams, quarrels and litigation. Much onyx is artificially stained. Cornelian is of a glowing orange-red. Cornelian beads are often imitated by glass, in which bubbles are always present.

Jasper is chalcedony adulterated with clayey materials. A red variety is particularly attractive. Banded jasper is striped with dull-green and maroon. Bloodstone is dark-green jasper with red spots which are said to have dropped on the stone from Christ's wounds as He hung on the Cross.

Chrysoprase is an apple-green translucent stone from Silesia. Rose quartz is of a cloudy translucent pink. Crocidolite, or tiger's eye, contains fibres of asbestos, resulting in a golden-brown sheen. Grey stones are called hawk's eye. The source is Griqualand West, South Africa.

Quartz crystal (1) uncut chalcedony (2) aventurine (3) Venus hair stone (4) cut citrine (5) moss agate (6) tree agate (7) chrysoprase (8) onyx (9) cornelian (10) bloodstone (11) tiger's eye (12)

Opal

Opal is a non-crystalline jelly of hydrated silica. The characteristic play of colour is caused by defraction, although not all opals display this phenomenon. Time will age some opals, driving off their essential moisture and causing them to shrink and crack.

Today most opal comes from Queensland or New South Wales. Black opal, most precious of all, comes from Lightning Ridge. These Australian stones often occur as *pseudomorphs*; shells and the bones of dinosaurs become encased in sandstone and in the course of time these rot away leaving a mould-like cavity into which liquid silica enters. The result is a perfect cast of a mollusc, or even a crystal of glaubers salt, in precious opal. Fire-opal comes from Mexico. It is usually quite transparent and of an orange colour. Mexican opal is usually faceted. Nowadays some opals are stained in the same way as onyx. The hardness of all opal is low – $5\frac{1}{2}$ to $6\frac{1}{2}$.

Jade

The term jade covers two quite different minerals, jadeite and nephrite. Jadeite, the more valuable, comes from Burma. Emerald-green is the most highly valued colour. Lavender, red, brown, white and black also occur. Although jadeite is not particularly hard, it is very tough due to its felt-like structure of minute, interlocked crystals. Variations in hardness cause softer portions of the stone to be undercut in the polishing process, causing a characteristic 'lemon-peel' surface.

Nephrite is typically green, a dark variety mottled with black being called spinach-jade, and an off-white kind, mutton-fat. Siberia and Turkestan are the principal sources of nephrite, but it also occurs in New Zealand.

Jades are often imitated by a blotchy green glass, but this mottling is more clearly defined than in the real thing. Bowenite is a green mineral similar in appearance to jade, but just soft enough to be marked with a file. Flakes of white chlorite are usually to be seen in this translucent material.

Uncut opal (1) two pseudomorphs (2, 3) white opal (4) black opal (5) fire opal (6) sectioned jadeite pebble (7) carved Chinese jade pendant (8)

1

2

3

4

5

7

8

6

Rare gems: axinite (1) sphene (2) kunzite (3)

Rare Gems

Some gems are so rare that one seldom finds them in jewellery and some are never seen outside museums and private collections. No cabinet of gems is considered complete without a sphene, a green, yellow, or brown stone of exceptional brilliance from Switzerland. Spodumene occurs in two varieties, pink kunzite which makes an occasional appearance in jewellery, and bright green hiddenite which is very rare, being found only as small stones from one locality in North Carolina. Benitoite is a blue stone of similar rarity, also from the United States. Iolite appears blue from only one direction, its dichroism being so strong that the colour fades to pale yellow as the stone is turned. Enstatite is a green stone from the South African diamond gravels. Both axinite and andalusite are brown in colour.

Obsidian, although by no means rare, seldom occurs in European jewellery. This is a black volcanic glass, occasionally with a gold or silver sheen due to partial crystallisation. Some natural glasses are of extra-terrestial origin. Nodules of such material found in the Australian deserts have been called 'black fellow's buttons' due to the curious forms they have taken in their journey through space.

Rhodonite

This is a pink opaque stone marked with black and found in the Ural mountains. Rough crystals are also found in New Jersey, in the United States. It is one of the silicate minerals and is of hardness $5\frac{1}{2}$–$6\frac{1}{2}$.

Malachite

Malachite is found where copper is mined, especially in the Urals. The Russians made luxuriant use of this stone, and furniture, and even the walls of large rooms were completely overlaid with slabs of it. Malachite is of hardness $3\frac{1}{2}$–4. It is also found in South Australia and in Arizona in the United States.

Lapis Lazuli

Lapis lazuli, an opaque mineral of a deep blue colour, is probably the sapphire referred to in the Old Testament. The finest material comes from Badakshan. Lapis lazuli is really a rock composed of three minerals, lazulite, haüynite, and sodalite, and is often scattered with golden flakes of iron pyrites. Simulants are: aventurine glass, a blue glass mingled with crystalline copper; and the so-called Swiss lapis, jasper stained with berlin blue and identified by pockets of crystalline quartz.

Malachite, uncut and cut and polished (1); cut rhodonite (2) cut lapis lazuli (3)

Pearls: white (1) black (2)
baroque (3) Mississippi (4)

Pearl

Although pearls are of organic origin, their structure is crystalline, composed of layers of calcium carbonate and conchiolin. When a grain of sand invades the oyster shell, irritation stimulates the mantle of the animal to pour out a fluid which encases the foreign material in nacre, leaving it as an excrescence on the lining of the shell. When the irritant is a small marine worm, however, the pearl forms in a cyst of mantle inside the body of the mollusc.

To culture pearls an incision is made in the mantle under aseptic conditions. A bead of freshwater mussel is inserted with a tiny graft of mantle, which, when the mollusc is returned to the sea, envelopes the bead completely, eventually covering it with nacre. Most cultured pearls come from Japan, but large pearls also come from Australia.

When the first cultured pearls appeared in the 1930s, prices collapsed, never to recover. Trading stopped overnight until some positive test could be discovered which would tell the two products of the oyster apart. X-rays are now in use to detect the mother-of-pearl core. Worm-like swellings, or a mirror-like flash from the bead core may betray a cultured pearl, although this is not a reliable guide.

Certain freshwater mussels produce pearls, but these lack the lustre of an oriental pearl. Pearls from the Mississippi river system are often of bizarre shapes. All irregular-shaped pearls are referred to as *baroque*.

Coral

Coral is the skeleton of a marine animal. Branch-like precious coral comes from the Mediterranean in shades of white, pink, and red. The centre of this trade is in Naples.

Jet

Jet is merely very hard coal and it burns quite readily. It is found at Whitby, Yorkshire, though a softer, inferior material comes from Asturias in Spain.

Amber

Amber is the fossil resin of pine trees which flourished in the Tertiary period. Much amber comes from the Baltic lands, and the centre of the trade is in Kaliningrad, Russia. Tradition affirmed that amber was the solidified urine of the lynx, dark from the male, pale from the female. Many shades of amber do exist: molasses-black with glittering gold fissures from Romania, beer-coloured with a fugitive blue glow from Sicily. Often insects are trapped in amber, perfectly preserved after millions of years. Real amber floats on very salt water, but glass and many plastic imitations sink.

Amber is a comparatively soft material, rating only $2\frac{1}{2}$ on the scale hardness. But it has been used as a material for jewels since ancient times.

Fly in amber pendant (1) jet necklace and pendant (2)

FAKES AND FORGERIES

From ancient times the very preciousness of jewellery has singled it out for imitation. But these early attempts were aimed more at simulating the material rather than the jewels. It is only in comparatively modern times that jewels have come to be valued for their age, and most forgeries are therefore of fairly recent date.

The presentation of a great forgery is usually planned with sophistication. In Vienna in the 1880s, the connoisseurs Count Wilczek and Baron Rothschild were approached by an unknown Romanian who had a magnificent gold tiara for sale. His story was that the tiara was a presentation by the citizens of Olbia, a Greek colony in southern Russia, to the Scythian king Saitaphernes. The noblemen decided to buy the crown for the Austrian Museum of Arts and Crafts, but the shrewd directors dissuaded them, having noted that the piece was in an almost miraculous state of preservation. However, the experts of the Louvre were convinced to the tune of 200,000 gold francs. Eventually from Odessa came the news that two Romanians had been commissioning works of art from pictorial references. The tiara of Saitaphernes was from the hand of Israel Ruchomovsky, an Odessa goldsmith!

William Smith and Charles Eaton inhabited a different world; the riverside London of the nineteenth century. Both earned their living scavenging on the Thames foreshore, at low water, but the handsome prices obtained for lead pilgrim badges pointed out their true vocation. In one year they found and sold 1,100 such objects to one dealer alone. At last the truth was told. The 'finds' came not from the bed of the Thames but from a house in Rosemary Street, close to the Tower. The medallions were characterised by a jumble of meaningless letters around their circumference. Some of the most learned archaeologists had been taken in by two illiterate men.

Today copies of the rose-diamond jewellery of the eighteenth century are made in Holland, and it takes a practised eye to detect them. The same cannot be said for the silver-gilt and enamel 'Renaissance' jewels made in Vienna.

Tiara of Saitaphernes (1) 'Billy and Charley' medallions (2)

EUROPEAN GOLD ASSAY MARKS

In most European countries gold and silver wares are punched
with an assay mark which indicates the purity of the metal.
Standards are counted in parts in a thousand (for example 920,
840, 750, 585), or, as in Britain, in carats (22 ct, 18 ct, 14 ct,

Austria from 1921, ·986 standard

Austria from 1921, ·585 standard

Belgium 1869–1939, ·750
standard

Belgium from 1942, ·750
standard

Denmark from 1893, ·585
standard

Finland from 1810

France from 1847

Germany from 1884

Hungary from 1937, ·750
standard

Hungary from 1937, ·585
standard

Italy from 1935

Poland from 1931

9 ct), 24 ct representing pure gold. Assay marks also give useful information about the time and place of manufacture. The following is a selection of European gold assay marks of the nineteenth to early twentieth centuries. British marks are too complex to be dealt with adequately here and detailed information about them can easily be found.

Portugal from 1938; jewellery

Spain from 1934, ·750 standard

Portugal from 1938; filigree

Spain from 1934, ·585 standard

Portugal from 1938; export

Sweden, state mark from 1901

Portugal from 1938; white gold

Sweden, Stockholm mark from 1759

Russia from 1861, ·583 standard

Turkey

GLOSSARY

À jour, open like lace

Baroque pearl, a pearl of irregular shape

Basse taille, a design flooded with translucent enamel

Beryl, emerald and aquamarine are varieties of this mineral

Bezel, the upper part of a ring, usually holding the stone

Blue white, the purest white seen in a diamond

Cameo, shell or stone carved with a design in relief

Cape, the straw colour sometimes seen in a diamond

Cat's eye, a cabochon stone showing a reflected line of light, as seen, for example, in quartz and chrysoberyl

Champlevé, enamel laid in cavities scooped out of the solid metal

Chasing, a decorative technique in which the design is traced out by blows of a punch from the front

Châtelaine, matching accessories, such as a watch or étui suspended from a decorative plate designed to hook on the belt

Chatoyancy, the cat's eye effect

Cinnamon, the dark brown colour sometimes seen in a diamond

Cleavage, a tendency of some crystals to split in one or more well-defined planes

Cloisonné, stones or enamels contained in metal cells

Coloured stones, precious stones except diamonds

Corundum, ruby and sapphire are varieties of this mineral

Croix à la Jeannette, a traditional French jewel, usually a cross suspended from a heart

Crown, the upper part of a faceted stone

Culet, the apex of the pavilion of a stone

Doublet, an imitation gemstone of a composite nature, the top of which is of stone, usually garnet, and the bottom of glass

Electrum, a natural alloy of gold and silver

Émail en résille sur verre, a type of enamelling on glass or crystal practised in the seventeenth century

Enseigne, a Renaissance cap badge

Eternity ring, a simple hoop with stones mounted all the way round

Facet, a plane surface on a

gemstone which has been cut to reflect light

Filigree, delicate and decorative wire-work

Foil, tinted metal sheet placed behind gemstones to enhance their colour

Girandole, a type of earring with three or more pendants

Granulation, minute spheres of metal applied to a surface to produce a decorative effect

Intaglio, an engraved stone, the design being sunk into its surface

Lapidary, one who cuts precious stones except diamonds

Lavallière, the American term for a negligé

Matrix, the rock in which a gemstone forms

Mêlée, diamonds of small size

Memento mori, a reminder of human mortality

Negligé, a simple pendant of singly mounted stones

Niello, a composition of sulphur, silver and other metals used like enamel and of a metallic black appearance

Orient, the lustre of a pearl

Paste, glass used to imitate precious stones

Pavé-set, set closely together in the style of paving

Pavilion, the lower part of a faceted stone usually concealed by the setting

Plique à jour, unbacked enamelwork through which the light passes like a stained-glass window

Pomander, a hollow sphere for holding perfume

Repoussé, a decorative technique in which the design is hammered out from the back of a thin sheet of gold

Schiller, the sheen seen in moonstone

Shank, the hoop of a ring

Silk, a silvery flash seen in rubies and sapphires and caused by closely massed fibrous crystals of rutile

Solitaire, a ring mounted with a single stone

Soudé emerald, two pieces of quartz or colourless beryl bonded together with clear green cement

Swiss lapis, jasper stained blue

Table, the facet on top of a stone

Verre églomisé, a painting in lacquer and gold leaf on the back of a glass plaque, which is intended to be viewed from the front through the glass

BOOKS TO READ

A Book of Jewels by J. & A. Bauer. Paul Hamlyn, 1966.

A History of Jewellery, 1100–1870 by Joan Evans. Faber, London, 1953.

English Victorian Jewellery by Ernle Bradford. Spring Books, 1967.

Four Centuries of European Jewellery by Ernle Bradford. Spring Books, 1967.

Gemmologists' Compendium by Robert Webster. N.A.G. Press Ltd., 1964.

Gemstones by G. F. Herbert Smith. Methuen, 1958.

Greek and Roman Jewellery by R. A. Higgins. Methuen, 1962.

Jewellery by H. Clifford Smith. Methuen, 1908.

Les Poinçons de Garantie internationaux pour l'Or by Tardy. Paris, Tardy, 1958.

Modern Design in Jewellery and Fans edited by Charles Holme. The Studio, 1902.

Modern Jewellery by Graham Hughes. Studio Vista, 1968.

Silverwork and Jewellery by Henry Wilson. Pitman, 1966.

Victorian Jewellery by M. Flower. Cassell, 1967.

INDEX

Page numbers in **bold** type refer to illustrations.

SOME OTHER TITLES IN THIS SERIES

- Arts
- Domestic Animals and Pets
- Domestic Science
- Gardening
- General Information
- History and Mythology
- Natural History
- Popular Science

Arts
Antique Furniture/Architecture/Clocks and Watches/Glass for Collectors/Jewellery/Musical Instruments/Porcelain/Pottery/Victoriana

Domestic Animals and Pets
Budgerigars/Cats/Dog Care/Dogs/Horses and Ponies/Pet Birds/Pets for Children/Tropical Freshwater Aquaria/Tropical Marine Aquaria

Domestic Science
Flower Arranging

Gardening
Chrysanthemums/Garden Flowers/Garden Shrubs/House Plants/Plants for Small Gardens/Roses

General Information
Aircraft/Arms and Armour/Coins and Medals/Flags/Fortune Telling/Freshwater Fishing/Guns/Military Uniforms/Motor Boats and Boating/National Costumes of the World/Orders and Decorations/Rockets and Missiles/Sailing/Sailing Ships and Sailing Craft/Sea Fishing/Trains/Veteran and Vintage Cars/Warships

History and Mythology
Age of Shakespeare/Archaeology/Discovery of: Africa/The American West/Australia/Japan/North America/South America/Great Land Battles/Great Naval Battles/Myths and Legends of: Africa/Ancient Egypt/Ancient Greece/Ancient Rome/India/The South Seas/Witchcraft and Black Magic

Natural History
The Animal Kingdom/Animals of Australia and New Zealand/Animals of Southern Asia/Bird Behaviour/Birds of Prey/Butterflies/Evolution of Life/Fishes of the world/Fossil Man/A Guide to the Seashore/Life in the Sea/Mammals of the world/Monkeys and Apes/Natural History Collecting/The Plant Kingdom/Prehistoric Animals/Seabirds/Seashells/Snakes of the world/Trees of the world/Tropical Birds/Wild Cats

Popular Science
Astronomy/Atomic Energy/Chemistry/Computers at Work/The Earth/Electricity/Electronics/Exploring the Planets/Heredity/The Human Body/Mathematics/Microscopes and Microscopic Life/Physics/Undersea Exploration/The Weather Guide